**Books are to be returned on or before
the last date below.**

ESSAYS
ON
ECONOMIC DEVELOPMENT

ESSAYS
ON
ECONOMIC DEVELOPMENT

BY

SHIGETO TSURU

ECONOMIC RESEARCH SERIES
No. 9
THE INSTITUTE OF ECONOMIC RESEARCH
HITOTSUBASHI UNIVERSITY

KINOKUNIYA BOOKSTORE CO., LTD.
Tokyo, Japan

D
330.952
TSU

Printed by
Kato Bummeisha Printing Co., Ltd.
Tokyo, Japan

PREFACE

Ever since my graduate student days at Harvard in 1930's I have kept my keen interest in the problem of economic development especially in its theoretical aspect. When, however, this topic came into vogue in the postwar period and relevant theories became ramified, refined and sharpened, I could not quite throw myself into the mainstream. There always remained in the back of my mind a hard core of scepticism toward the dominant trend of development theories which abstracted from differences in social systems.

The first occasion which confronted me with the mainstream occurred during my brief sojourn in Bangkok in 1955 when I served as economic affairs officer with the Economic Commission for Asia and the Far East. A large majority of economists then associated with the United Nations contended that developing countries could achieve a high rate of growth, at least in the short run, by attempting to "reduce the over-all capital-output ratio" for which purpose the emphasis on those industries with lowest sectoral capital-output ratios would be called for. I could not be persuaded with this position even as a matter of short-run recommendation and wrote a memorandum to be circulated within the office. This memorandum became the basis for an essay which is here reproduced as Chapter One.

A large number of critical essays I have written since that time, usually in Japanese, are fairly well represented in this volume. In each one of them, I think readers will note my propensity to drag the problem somehow into the dimension of historical relations where *differentia specifica* of a particular mode of production play an important role. I am aware that this methodological propensity of mine bids me, for its fulfilment, to essay a positive, rather than merely critical, interpretation of the process of economic development (of, for example, Japan) weaving into that analysis the efficacy of my own method of approach. I am at present engaged in such a work, and the essay included here as Chapter Seven ("The Take-Off of Japan, 1868–1900") might be regarded as a sort of connecting link between this volume and the project under way.

Japan happens to provide a peculiarly interesting case from the standpoint of both the "take-off" type of analysis and the growth analysis of a developed economy. In particular, the record of sustained growth-rate of more than nine percent per annum for over a decade after the postwar rehabilitation was more or less completed is a performance which challenges economists for explanation. I have made an attempt at such explanation in the latter chapters of Part Two; but here, too, some readers may regard my emphasis on non-economic matters as somewhat unorthodox. The last chapter of this volume gives an inkling of my concern on "costs of economic growth" —the costs which I am certain will attract greater and greater attention as the time goes on.

All the essays included here were made public in one form or another during the period between 1956 and 1964. I have indicated at the beginning of each chapter the specific circumstance which provided me occasion for writing it; and I should like to take this opportunity to register my gratitude for the permissions granted for reproduction by the publications concerned.

Tokyo, 1968

SHIGETO TSURU

CONTENTS

CONTENTS

II. JAPAN'S EXPERIENCE

I. THEORETICAL

Chapter 1

A NOTE ON CAPITAL-OUTPUT RATIO[1]

[1956]

This essay grew out of the discussion with some expert members of the Economic Commission for Asia and the Far East while the author was serving there as economic affairs officer in the fall of 1955 and was subsequently published in an article form in *Keizai Kenkyu*, April 1956. It is here reprinted without revision.

1.   The following symbols and definitions will be used throughout this paper:

K......the existing stocks of durable producers' structures and equipment (D) plus inventories (S)

Y......the current flow of income (or output)

I......the current net addition of K, or ΔK, or $\Delta D + \Delta S$

y......the additional flow of income (or output) yielded from net investment

k......the average capital/output ratio, or K/Y

k'......the marginal capital/output ratio, or investment/output ratio, or I/y

[1] In the course of preparing this paper, the writer is indebted to Drs. H.W. Singer, A.K. Ghosh and Ashok Mitra for helpful suggestions.

2. What is commonly called "capital/output ratio" nowadays has several antecedents with differing implications and applications. Sometimes it has been used in its reciprocal form and called "product/capital ratio" or "the productivity of capital." Further, it has definite affinities to such concepts as "period of production," "turn-over of capital," "organic composition of capital," and "accelerator." Without going into too refined a discussion on the subject, we may classify the use of these affiliated concepts into the following three classes:

(1) As measuring the *average life of capital goods in use*: R.W. Goldsmith, for example, who made calculations of average and marginal capital/output ratios for the United States annually over 1897–1950, says that "the actual level of the ratios is determined by the fact that in static conditions the overall ratio is equal to one-half the average life of total output."[2] W.A. Lewis' formulation of the concept also comes to the same thing as that of Goldsmith, although his wording appears to be different from that of the latter. Lewis says: "In the mathematical sense the ratio of the existing stock of capital to income (i.e. the average as distinct from the marginal ratio) is simply a function of the proportion of national income invested, the average life of investments, and the rate of growth of income."[3] From this, he naturally goes on to say that "given the average life of capital, the principal determinant of the capital-income ratio is the proportion of national income annually invested."[4] This implies that, instead of writing an equation like $GC = s$, it is more appropriate to regard the rate of growth as determined by the average life of capital and the rate of investment.

[2] International Association for Research in Income and Wealth, *Income and Wealth*, Series II, 1952, p. 298, footnote.

[3] W.A. Lewis, *The Theory of Economic Growth*, 1955, p. 202.

[4] *Ibid.*, p. 202.

(2) As measuring the *relation of incremental output to induced investment:* This is the relation visualized as proceeding from ΔY to I and most commonly identified with the term "accelarator."[5] Although there are many variations in this application, almost all of them use the concept in the marginal sense and conceive of I here as theoretically-induced magnitude, most typically exemplified by Harrod's C_r which is defined as "the requirement for new capital divided by the increment of output to sustain which the new capital is required."[6] The commonest use of the concept in this sense has been in the sphere of trade cycle theory and a great deal of refinements have been carried out in the past several years.

(3) As measuring *the productivity of capital:* Here again the concept is generally used in the marginal sense, but proceeding from a given I to the additional flow of net output yielded from that investment, or y according to our notation. Whereas in the use of the concept measuring the relation of incremental output to induced investment the latter is conceived as a *theoretically*-induced magnitude, the concept as used in the sense of the productivity of capital would require the additional flow of net output to be conceived as a *theoretically*-derived magnitude. That is the reason why a special notation, y, is used in this paper instead of ΔY. Theoretically, the concept in this sense has been made much use of by E. Domar in its reciprocal form, and more lately by a large number of economists who are concerned with the investment programming in under-developed economies.

[5] The accelerator, of course, usually relates the rate of change of consumer demand to the derived demand for investment, whereas the capital/output in this application relates, generally speaking, the rate of change of total output, ΔY, to investment.
[6] R.F. Harrod, *Towards a Dynamic Economics*, 1948, p. 82.

The purpose of this paper is to examine the concept of capital/output ratio especially in relation to the last use mentioned, namely as a theoretical and practical instrument of investment programming.

3. In applying the concept of capital/output ratio to the investment programming of under-developed economies, there seems to be an accepted body of opinion which is best represented by a recent study by the United Nations Secretariat, "Problems and Techniques of Economic Development Planning and Programming with Special Reference to ECAFE Countries."[7] The study sets out a general proposition as follows: "The rate of economic growth may be analytically considered as being the function of two factors, (a) the rate of capital formation and (b) the captal/output ratio; accordingly, development policies may be described as aiming to increase the former, reduce the latter, or do both."[8] Here, the "capital/output ratio" is defined as "the relationship between the net capital formation of a certain time period and the additional net output that results in the first subsequent time period in which the effects of that capital formation can be fully felt,"[9] although for practical purposes it is proposeed to use the ratio in the form of "the relationship between increment of capital and increment of output, both in the *same* period."[10] In other words, it is suggested that it is desirable to reduce k' (according to our notation) if we wish to speed up the growth rate of an economy and that since k' in the theoretical sense is difficult to calculate an approximation might be made by computing the

7) *Economic Bulletin for Asia and the Far East*, Vol. VI, No. 3. November 1955.
8) *Ibid.*, pp. 25–6.
9) *Ibid.*, p. 26, footnote.
10) *Ibid.*

ratio between I and ΔY, or between investment and incremental output of the same period.

In the accepted body of opinion, to which reference has been made, the above general proposition is understood to imply that investment in industries with low capital / output ratios is preferable in those economies where the rate of capital formation is still low. In such discussions it is usually taken for granted that k' could be used in sectoral sense and further that a high sectoral k' is equivalent to a high degree of capital intensity. The statement that an under-developed economy with a large population and a low rate of saving had better emphasize, in its initial stage of economic development, investment in the so-called "quick-yielding projects" such as agricultural development rather than in "capital intensive" projects such as steel industry or ship-building is usually based upon the reasoning summarized here. Naturally, in so far as the tool of programming itself, i.e. k', either in its overall or sectoral sense, can not be isolated from various contingencies of the actual world, the proposition in question is accompanied by an array of qualifications.[11] But the essence of the matter is regarded as unimpaired by these qualifications.

4. It cannot be doubted that as a matter of abstract

[11] For example, the study by U.N. Secretariat quoted above surrounds the general proposition with such qualifications as follows: "Quick-maturing projects obviously offer relatively lower capital/output ratios from the immediate point of view, but not necessarily a lower ratio when a longer period is considered. The time element plays a key role in the concept of capital/output ratio used as an investment criterion." (*Ibid.*, p. 44) "When applying the criterion of capital/output ratios to specific investment projects or specific sectors, the supplementary benefits of any project to other economic activities should be considered, although these cannot easily be measured." (p. 44) "In a way, the lowering of the present capital/output ratio conflicts with the creation of a capital base for the economy, which is likely to involve relatively capital-intensive investment." (p. 44) And so on.

principle it is true to say that the rate of growth of an economy depends upon its rate of capital formation and the overall investment/output ratio. But when this proposition is applied to the investment programming of an under-developed economy, there seem to crop up a number of confusions which could be traced to a somewhat superficial use of the term "capital/output ratio." An attempt will be made, therefore, in this paragraph, to bring out the basic theoretical implications of the overall investment/output ratio, or k', with an aid of a simple model.

Let there be two industries, the investment industry (with subscript i) and the consumer goods industry (with subscript c). Assume the productivity (in the sense of the quantity of product per unit labor) of p_i and p_c, with the labor power engaged of L_i and L_c, respectively. Assume also the common wage rate of w (per unit labor) for both sectors. For simplicity's sake, it is further assumed that workers consume all of their income, that profits (Π) arise only in the consumer goods industry, and that all the profits are invested. Then:

Consumer goods produced: $p_c L_c = w L_c + \Pi$

Investment: $(p_c - w) L_c = w L_i$

These expressions are in units of consumer goods; but investment in units of own goods can be written: $p_i L_i$. If we assume the labor coefficient of a per investment good when the latter is applied in the production of consumer goods, $p_i L_i$ units of investment will require $a p_i L_i$ units of labor power, and will result in the production of $a p_i L_i$-times-p_c units of consumer goods.[12]

Under these simplified assumptions, the investment/output

---

[12] p_c and p_i are likely to move in the opposite direction. The progress in technology usually implies that the increase in p_c more than makes up for the reduction in p_i.

ratio, or k', can be written as follows:

$$k' = \frac{wL_i}{ap_cp_iL_i} = \frac{w}{ap_cp_i} \tag{1}$$

In other words, the investment/output ratio comes to be an expression where the wage rate appears in the numerator and a combined index of productivities appears in the denominator. If the wage rate is kept constant while productivities rise, the investment/output ratio will be reduced. If the wage rate keeps pace with the rise in productivities, the investment/output ratio will not change. Such an implication is quite consistent with the proposition that given the rate of capital formation the growth-rate of an economy is larger when the investment/output ratio is smaller. But the same thing can be stated much more directly by saying that the growth-rate will be larger when the wage rate can be kept lagging behind the rise in productivity. Instead of saying that it is desirable to lower the investment/output ratio, we could point directly to factors involved and formulate the wage policy appropriate to the growth pattern desired. It might well be that the fact that the average capital/output ratio has remained almost constant for a long time in countries like the U.K. and the U.S.A. in spite of the almost certain rise in productivities is explained by the concomitant rise in the real wage rate. And again, the fact that the capital/output ratio of U.S.S.R. is said to have been quite low for some time (a little less than two according to Professor Mahalanobis) could be explained in terms of the deliberate policy of keeping wage rate constant while productivities rose. Thus, the relevence of wage policy (or its allied problems) to the development planning seems to require a greater degree of attention than given, for example, in the U.N. Secretariat study referred to earlier.

It must be noted, however, that in a free competitive economy the wage rate (w) and the productivity of labor (p_c) are not independent of each other. In other words, the numerator and the denominator of the expression (1) can be a separate object of deliberate policy only to a limited extent. But what is important is to be aware of the essential factors involved when we make use of the concept like the investment/output ratio. Usefulness of the formulation like (1) might be indicated further by relinquishing one of the simplifying assumptions, i.e., that of the common wage rate. Suppose now that the wage rate in the consumer goods industry is w_c and that in the investment goods industry w_i, and that both I and y are to be expressed in terms of w_c.

Then:

$$k' = \frac{w_i L_i / w_c}{a p_c p_i L_i / w_c} = \frac{w_i}{w_c} \cdot \frac{w_c}{a p_c p_i}$$

Suppose $w_i > w_c$ and $\dfrac{w_i - w_c}{w_c} = \delta$, then:

$$k' = (l + \delta) \cdot \frac{w_c}{a p_c p_i} \tag{2}$$

This expression implies that k' can be lowered by reducing δ, or the wage differential between the consumer goods industry and the investment goods industy. In actual application this point can be interpreted as suggesting that an under-developed economy which is dependent on the importation of capital goods from a high-wage economy could lower k' by learning to produce the same capital goods at home with its own labor.

5. The expression like (1) which has been arrived at on the basis of a simplified model may sound somewhat accidental. But it is by no means the case. That it expresses the essential

content of the concept like capital/output ratio can be shown by adopting a different approach.

Let us start with the concept of subsistence fund in Böhm-Bawerk. In his formulation, the subsistence-fund, F, which is required to enable production in a roundabout manner extending over N years is equal to $(1+N)$ times the annual wage-bill, W, divided by two, or[13]

$$F=\frac{(1+N)W}{2} \tag{3}$$

Assumptions which underlie this formulation can be made less arbitrary in two respects, i.e., (a) the discrete stage of production which Böhm-Bawerk visualized can be changed into a continuous one, that is, a stage of one year can be broken into stages of $1/n$ years with n approaching to infinity; and (b) the unilaterally moving structure of production which Böhm-Bawerk assumed can be changed into a more general one where capital goods will be assumed to be used not only for the production of consumer goods but for the production of capital goods themselves. By adopting the first of the above two modifications, we can rewrite the equation (3) into a simpler form: $F=\frac{NW}{2}$.[14] The right-hand side of this equation can be rewritten as $\frac{N}{2} \cdot wL$ in which w stands for the wage rate and L for the labor employed. Now, $\frac{N}{2} \cdot L$ in this expression is found to be equal to the total of labor power applied in

---

[13] For the discussion in this paragraph, the writer owes greatly to Kei Shibata, *Shin Keizai Ronri* (A New Logic of Economics), 1942, pp. 20–26.

[14] First, we can rewrite the equation (3) as follows: $F=(1+nN)\dfrac{W}{2n}$. Then, if n approaches infinity, this becomes $F=\left(\dfrac{1}{\infty}+N\right)\dfrac{W}{2}=\dfrac{NW}{2}$.

all the stages of production appropriately weighted by respective period of gestation. For, in the Böhm-Bawerkian scheme, such a total should be equal to the quantity of labor power applied in each stage of production (which we may represent by a) multiplied by $(1+2+3+\ldots\ldots+N)$, or $\frac{(a+N)N}{2}$, and when the time period is taken infinitesimally, it becomes $aN^2/2$ which is equivalent to $\frac{N}{2}$ times $aN\ (=L)$.

The experssion $\frac{N}{2}.L$ (the total of labor power applied in all the stages of production appropriately weighted by respective period of gestation) will take a different form when we incorporate the second of modifications mentioned above, that is to say, when we assume that capital goods are used not only for the production of consumer goods but also for the production of capital goods themselves. The simplest manner in which we can visualize such a situation will be to assume that there is only one capital good and one consumer good, the period of production for both being one year and each of which requiring for the production of one unit c units of capital goods $(c < 1)$ and a units of labor power. Under such an assumption the quantity of total labor required for the production of one unit of consumer good should be equal to $a(1+c+c^2+\ldots\ldots)$ or $\frac{a}{1-c}$, since c units of capital good needed for the production of one unit of consumer good require ac units of labor power and c^2 units of capital good, and these c^2 units of capital good require for their production ac^2 units of labor power and c^3 units of capital good, and so on. If we again make a summation to obtain the total of labor power applied in all the stages of production appropriately weighted by respective period of production, it comes to $a(1+2c+3c^2+4c^3+\ldots\ldots)=\frac{a}{(1-c)^2}$. This

12

quantity multiplied by wage rate w should give us the subsistence fund required for the reprodudtion of one unit of consumer good. Therefore, the total subsistence fund needed for the annual output of all the consumer goods (which we shall write as Q) can be expressed as follows:

$$F = \frac{awQ}{(1-c)^2} \qquad (4)$$

Since the total wage bill required is equal to the wage rate (w) times the labor power required per consumer good $\left(\frac{a}{1-c}\right)$ times the output of consumer good (Q), the roundaboutness that can be expressed by the ratio between the subsistence-fund and the total wage bill will be equal to:

$$\frac{awQ}{(1-c)^2} \div \frac{awQ}{(1-c)} = \frac{1}{1-c}$$

This should be equal to $\frac{N}{2}$ in the simpler formulation of Böhm-Bawerk, and let us designate this measure of roundaboutness of production by b, such that $b = \frac{a}{1-c}$. On the other hand, since $\frac{a}{1-c}$ is the amount of labor required in the production of one unit of consumer good, the productivity of labor in the sense of quantity of consumer goods produced by a unit of labor should be the reciprocal of $\frac{a}{1-c}$, or $\frac{1-c}{a}$. Let us designate this by m, such that $m = \frac{1-c}{a}$. Then the equation (4) can be rewritten as follows:

$$\frac{F}{Q} = \frac{w}{m} \cdot b \qquad (5)$$

The left-hand side of this equation is equivalent to the average capital/output ratio, and the right-hand side indicates that the

capital/output ratio is directly proportional to the wage rate
and the roundaboutness of production and is inversely proportional to the productivity of labor. This is the relationship
which is quite similar to that revealed in the equation (1).
Although there are certain differences in the concepts employed
between the formulation which resulted in the equation (1) and
that given here, the essential implication of a concept like
capital/output ratio is revealed in both and can be expressed
in the form of a function of the wage rate-divided by-product-
ivity, or w/m in (5).

6. The next problem to be dealt with is the relation
between the investment/output ratio and the degree of capital
intensity. As has been pointed out earlier, a widely accepted
body of opinion as regards the investment programming of
under-developed economies usually identifies the high invest-
ment/output ratio with the high degree of capital intensity,
using both concepts in the sectoral sense as in the overall.

There is no objection to using the *average* capital/output ratio
in the sectoral sense, so long as we are aware of the specific
limitations of the concept in a particular application. Using
the subscript i to indicate the sectoral use of various categories,
we may write:

$$k_i = \frac{D_i + S_i}{Y_i}$$

where Y_i may be regarded as the sum of wage payments in
that sector (W_i) and the surplus value arising in that sector
(Π_i). The average capital/output ratio in this formulation is,
no doubt, quite similar to the concept of the degree of capital
intensity, which may be designated by d and written as:

14

$$d_i = \frac{D_i}{W_i}$$

or the ratio of durable producers' structure and equipment employed in a certain sector and the wages-bill paid in that sector. If we write the relative share of workers in the new value created as η, such that $W = \eta Y$, we could easily relate the average capital/output ratio to the degree of capital intensity as follows:

$$k_i = \frac{D_i + S_i}{Y_i} = \frac{D_i}{Y_i} + \frac{S_i}{Y_i} = \eta d_i + \frac{S_i}{Y_i}$$

from which we may say that if inventories occupy a constant proportion of output and the relative share of workers remains unchanged, the average capital/output ratio will be roughly proportional to the degree of capital intensity.

The degree of capital intensity as formulated in this manner is essentially a sectoral concept and has its uses in economic analysis. But can we speak of a sectoral k', or a sectoral investment/output ratio? To the extent the economy is integrated in such a way that all the sectors are interrelated to each other, investment in any one sector will materialize itself in final output to which all the sectors contribute; and it will be difficult to speak of a sectoral k'. Take, for example, a new investment in cotton-spinning industry to the amount of I_c which can be associated with the increase in the value added in that industry to the amount of y_c. It is important to note in this case that y_c can be realized only if there goes on antecedent or concomitant expansion in, say, the spinning machine industry *and* if it does not conflict with the concomitant investment in the competing industry, such as synthetic fibres. One could, if one wishes, refer to I_c/y_c as the investment/output ratio of the cotton spinning industry, but such a ratio could hardly be used as a criterion for investment decisions. It seems that if one wishes to use k' in the sense of reciprocal of productivity of investment, one has to confine the use of k' only in an overall sense except where a certain sector can be ascertained to be independent from other sectors.

Furthermore, it is quite *possible* that the overall investment/output ratio is lowered through the development of an industry with a high degree of capital intensity. This is *a priori* evident from the essential implication of the investment/output ratio developed earlier. Maurice Dobb has discussed this question extensively,[15] and we do not propose to go into the subject in this Note. It is only necessary to add that the concept of "capital" has been used in so many different meanings in the recent past and that it is about time that we make appropriate distinctions among, for example, capital in the sense of durable producers' structure and equipment, capital in the sense of a counterpart to saving (which could easily be an increase in inventories only as in the Marxian model of extended reproduction), capital in the sense of subsistence fund as in Böhm-Bawerk, and so on.

[15] Maurice Dobb, "A Note on the so-called Degree of Capital-intensity of Investment in Under-developed Countries," *On Economic Theory and Socialism*, 1955, pp. 138–154.

Chapter 2

THE APPLICABILITY AND LIMITATIONS OF ECONOMIC DEVELOPMENT THEORY

[1958]

This essay represents a revision and expansion of the author's earlier English article, "Some Theoretical Doubts on India's Plan-Frame," *Economic Weekly* (Bombay), January 1957. The original Japanese version was included in the volume of essays entitled *Keizai no Ronri to Genjitsu* (*Logic and Reality in Economics*), 1959; and the translation was done by Mr. C.S. Khang, revised by Messrs. M. Bronfenbrenner and H. Kanemitsu, as a project of the University of Minnesota-Ford Foundation Workshop in Economic Development and was published in *The Indian Economic Journal*, April 1962. It is here reprinted with the author's revision on translation.

I

Studies of economic development problems have flourished to such an extent in the postwar period that it is difficult even to classify them in any systematic order. Many of these studies have examined their problems by constructing theoretical models. Since the economic development of underdeveloped countries is a real-world problem, the validity of specific theories can actually be tested. Even though it may be difficult to test the validity of a particular theory in practice, we can at least examine the soundness of its conceptual framework and the validity of the approach adopted in its construction. This paper is intended to examine these theories.

The most important point in contemporary development theories is the manner of allocating scarce capital resources most efficiently between the various sectors of an economy. This scarcity of capital is only a common-sense starting-point. It is easy to find the following vicious circle in reality: Under-development of an economy → low Gross National Product → low saving → low investment → low economic growth rate → low Gross National Product. Thus, there seems to be in principle not much room to argue against a view that a nation should borrow new capital from abroad, or should attempt to increase its Gross National Product by using more effectively the small amount of its domestic savings.

However, problems in reality are not quite so simple. It is very difficult to construct a satisfactory theoretical model even within the limitation of development theories which abstract from differences in social systems. In order to clarify this point, we shall begin by examining the theoretical model which formed the basis of India's Second Five-Year Plan. This model originated in the Indian Statistical Institute under the leadership of Professor Mahalanobis. It was subjected to preliminary studies by many distinguished economists, including Bettelheim of France, Lange of Poland, Goodwin of England, Tinbergen of the Netherlands, Degtyar and Pisarev of the U.S.S.R., Galbraith of the U.S.A., and so on. But the final decisions and responsibilities apparently lay with Mahalanobis himself,[1] and the model is usually referred to as the "Plan-Frame." Starting from an abstract, simple model, it was developed by degrees into a detailed one including numerous statistical estimates. Comparing the final statistical estimates of the "Plan-Frame" with the figures finally adopted in the Second Five-Year Plan, we find the two sets of figures almost identical. This leaves little doubt that the Five-Year Plan had started with the Mahalanobis' theoretical model as its basis.

II

The Mahalanobis model can be explained in terms of a simple two-sector economy.

Its starting point is supplied by the Keynesian equation, $Y=C+K$, where Y is national income, C consumption, and K investment. This procedure divides the economy into C (consumption-goods) and K (investment-goods) sectors. Even though Mahalanobis did not take time to explain explicitly, we need to know what the two sectors represent. These two sectors (C and K) differ from the Marxian two-department partition. In the Marxian partition, producer goods and consumption goods are distinguished in terms of their use-values. For example, the producer goods needed to produce cunsumption goods are produced in the K sector. It does not matter whether producer goods are produced for expansion purposes or as replacements; so long as they are producer goods, they are produced in the producer-goods sector. Since, however, in the Keynesian sectoring of the economy, "investment goods" refer

[1] Cf. P.C. Mahalanobis, "The Approach of Operational Research to Planning in India," *Sankhyā* (December, 1955), pp. 3–62.

to the material content of new investment, the term "investment goods" means specifically new material installations plus increased inventories of raw materials and consumption goods. It is therefore impossible to define uniquely "the investment-goods sector" as "an economic activity." On the other hand, the consumption-goods sector subsumes replacement investment. Therefore this view regards the consumption-goods sector production as a completely integrated process. Hence it must be noted that Mahalanobis' consumption-goods sector differs from the "Department II" of the Marxian reproduction scheme.

Using this Keynesian sectoring of the economy, Mahalanobis goes on to state that from total net new investment λ_c fraction would be used for the expansion of the consumption sector and λ_k fraction for the expansion of the investment sector. Needless to say, $\lambda_c + \lambda_k = 1$. He also uses the coefficient β to represent the relation between new investment in any sector and the resulting increase in income produced by this sector; or,

$$\beta = \frac{\text{increase of income due to new investment}}{\text{amount of new investment}}$$

This β might be called the "productivity of investment," being the inverse of the usual marginal capital coefficient. The β coefficients may vary, even for one and the same industry, from one time to another and from one nation to another, but Mahalanobis has taken the position that for the duration of a five-year planning period these coefficients can be regarded as constant. Of course, there are separate β_c and β_k for the consumption and investment sectors respectively. In addition, let:

20

Y_0 = the initial year's national income
C_0 = ,, ,,   ,, consumption
K_0 = ,, ,,   ,, investment

and also:

$$\alpha_0 = K_0/Y_0$$

Then we have:

$$K_{t+1} - K_t = \lambda_k \beta_k K_t \tag{1.1}$$

$$C_{t+1} - C_t = \lambda_c \beta_c K_t \tag{1.2}$$

so that:

$$\beta_k = \frac{K_{t+1} - K_t}{\lambda_i K_t} \quad \text{and} \quad \beta_c = \frac{C_{t+1} - C_t}{\lambda_c K_t}$$

From these basic equations showing the expansion process of the two sectors, we can derive the following equations for K_t and Y_t, given K_0 and Y_0:

$$K_t = (1 + \lambda_k \beta_k)^t K_0 \tag{1.3}$$

$$Y_t = Y_0 \left[1 + \alpha_0 \frac{\lambda_k \beta_k + \lambda_c \beta_c}{\lambda_k \beta_k} \{(1 + \lambda_k \beta_k)^t - 1\} \right] \tag{1.4}$$

In these equations, λ_c and λ_k are called by Mahalanobis "allocation parameters," and are determined deliberately by the planning authorities based on planned allocations. On the other hand, β_c and β_k are given by the production situations of each sector. The problem is, then, posed how λ_c and λ_k could be determined in such a way that the planners' objectives can be fulfilled, such objectives, for example, as to maximize the growth rate of national income for a specified period of time, or to maximize the volume of employment absorbed again for a specified period of time, etc.. If we want to introduce employment as a variable, this can be done by using another parameter θ, which is the amount of new capital needed to employ an additional worker.

III

To make the foregoing simple model into a more concrete working one, Mahalanobis further subdivides the C sector into three subsectors; namely:

C_1......Consumption goods produced by modern factories.

C_2......Consumption goods produced by small- or medium-sized, and family-type factories.

C_3......Services.

Further, in relation to the actual plan, a number of concrete conditions, which also are the objectives of the plan, have to be met. For example:

1. Full or near-full employment, meaning an increase in employment of 11 million workers in five years. (We use N to represent the target increase in employment.)

2. A relatively high growth rate, approximately 5 per cent per annum.

3. Procurement of new investment funds, including inflow of foreign capital, amounting to Rs. 56 billion in five years; we shall denote this amount by A.

4. National income of the initial year (Y_0), estimated to be Rs. 108 billion. Then, if the growth rate is 5 per cent per annum, the total increase of national income in five years should be Rs. 29 billion, denoted by E.

In addition to these conditions, we must estimate coefficients such as the β's and θ's. Mahalanobis' estimates for them were as follows:

Sector	β	θ(Rs)
K	0.20	20,000
C_1	0.35	8,750
C_2	1.25	2,500
C_3	0.45	3,750

For example, if we make a new investment of Rs. 10,000 in sector C_1, the increase in income produced by this sector from this year to the next will be Rs. 3,500, and it would require Rs. 8,750 to increase employment in C_1 by one man. Since how these coefficients (especially β's) were estimated will be quite important in the latter part of this discussion, it is necessary to add a word as to the method of their estimation. Although in the First Five-Year Plan, the coefficient for "productivity of investment" was assumed *a priori* to be 0.33 for the entire economy, it was necessary for the Second to have empirical estimates for such coefficients inasmuch as different β's were desired for different sectors. In order to estimate these coefficients, we need to know not only to which sector various industries belong, but also the cost of replacing existing plant and equipment anew, since actual statistics refer to the capital stock which had been depreciated with the passage of time. If we adopt the stationary assumption that the value of existing capital instruments equals one-half the cost of replacing them with new ones, the theoretical values of β's will be one-half the values actually estimated. For example, $\beta_k = 0.2$ in the model. This is derived from an estimate that the actual average β_k for a sample of "capital goods" industry, within manufacturing (which is identified with "the investment goods sector"), was 0.43 in the period 1949–1953. For β_1, Mahalanobis used the average of the census figures for Indian manufacturing industries in the period 1946–1950, the observed

23

average being 0.6. Excluding those producing primarily capital goods, the figure was 0.7. Hence $\beta_1 = \frac{1}{2}(0.7) = 0.35$. For β_2, he used data from the National Income Survey and obtained the figure of 1.5, but he adjusted it downwards to 1.25 on the ground that the observed period was unusually bad years for agriculture on account of the unfavorable weather conditions. As for β_3, nothing more is said than that it was computed from data supplied by the Reserve Bank of India.

It also appears that the capital-labour ratios (θ's) were derived from reports of the Census of Manufactures and other specialized reports, using methods similar to those used in estimating the β–coefficients. In the estimation of θ_3, Mahalanobis said that his figure was estimated from data on expenditures and employment in education, public health, and transportation. This figure of Rs. 3,750 appears to be too small, and as will be remarked later, I have doubts about the basic data used.

Using the given conditions and the coefficients mentioned above, our problem can be set up as follows: Firstly, the allocation ratios of investment are:

$$\lambda_k + \lambda_1 + \lambda_2 + \lambda_3 = 1 \tag{2.1}$$

Secondly, the number of new employment expected has to be divided in accordance with the equation:

$$n_k + n_1 + n_2 + n_2 = N \tag{2.2}$$

Then, thirdly, the total of new investment for five years, designated as A, has to be equal to the sum of the amounts allocated to each sector, which amount being the product of the number to be newly employed (n's) and the capital-labor ratio (θ's). Thus:

$$n_k \theta_k + n_1 \theta_1 + n_2 \theta_2 + n_2 \theta_3 = A \tag{2.3}$$

24

Since the amount of investment $\lambda_i A$ in any sector equals the funds invested in that sector, $\lambda_i A = n_i \theta_i$, and hence equations (2.1) and (2.3) are identical. And finally, the total increase of national income over five years, designated as E, should be the sum of incomes created in the four sectors, each of which can be expressed as the product of "the productivity of investment" (β's) and the amount of investment allocated ($n\theta$'s). Thus:

$$\beta_k n_k \theta_k + \beta_1 n_1 \theta_1 + \beta_2 n_2 \theta_2 + \beta_3 n_3 \theta_3 = E \tag{2.4}$$

In the Mahalanobis model, λ_k is assumed to be 33 per cent. This condition is imposed, considering the necessary conditions for a satisfactory rate of economic growth, and there is no theoretical reason why it must be 33 per cent. Then, once we know the values for the λ_i, we can compute the n_i from the relation: $\lambda_i = (n_i \theta_i)/A$. Thus the problem is one of solving the above equations for λ_1, λ_2, and λ_3. Solving this system of equations, we obtain the solution presented in the following table:

Sector	Increase in Employment (Millions)	Allocation of Investment Funds (Rs. Million)	Increase in Income (Rs. Million)
K	0.9	18,500	3,700
C_1	1.1	9,800	3,400
C_2	4.7	11,800	14,700
C_3	4.3	16,000	7,200
Total	11.0	56,000	29,000

Mahalanobis goes on to divide further the C_2 sector into agriculture and the household indystry. But so far as the basic skeleton of the model is concerned, the above summary should suffice. What Mahalanobis asserts on the basis of the above is that the solution obtained as summarized in the foregoing table is in some sense "optimal." For example, he says that "with any given amount of total assets formation—

and with any given set of values of the β-coefficients—there would be, in principle, an optimum allocation of resources in relation to the basic objectives."[2]   Our next task is therefore to examine whether the values obtained in this solution should really be termed "optimal."

IV

The first point to be mentioned in connection with the characteristics of the model is the way the economy is partitioned.   As has been mentioned already, Mahalanobis partitions the economy by means of Keynesian aggregate concepts.   This method of partitioning an economy is of course quite common in current development theories, and so long as we are interested in purely theoretical analysis this sort of economic partition introduces no difficulties.   In particular, if we suppose that capital goods are non-depreciating permanent assets, we can describe each of consumption-goods and investment-goods sectors as representing a uniquely identifiable "economic activity."   But in practice it is well-nigh impossible to partition the economy by means of Keynesian *net* aggregate concepts. To simplify his problem, Mahalanobis classifies the steel and engineering industries as belonging to the investment-goods sector.   Conceptually speaking, however, part of machine production, which goes to replace depreciated capital stocks, should rather belong to the consumption-goods sector.   This sort of difficulty appears to have disturbed Mahalanobis somewhat, judging by his remark that "appropriate fractions of investment in industries manufacturing intermediate (producer) goods should be allocated to λ_k and λ_c in proportion to

[2] Mahalanobis, *op. cit.*, p. 46.

the value of such intermediate goods used in the capital goods (K-sector) and consumer goods (C-sector) industries respectively."[3] What he calls "capital goods" here, however, apparently refers to producers' durables, and so far as these goods are concerned, he seems to take the position that they belong entirely to the K-sector. Even when it is possible to partition the various industries into C and K sectors along strict Keynesian lines, or in fact the more strictly one attempts at such partitioning, all the more complex becomes the computation of the β's and θ's, so complex as to make it almost impossible to decide whether or not the solution itself provides an "optimal" resource allocation.

With special reference to β_k, we must know the theoretical meaning of this coefficient. For example, suppose that:

  100=National income (first year)
  85=Consumption (first year).
  15=Investment (first year).

$$\frac{\text{Capital}}{\text{coefficient}} = \frac{\text{New investment}}{\text{Increased income due to new investment}} = 2.5$$

Then β (for the entire economy) $= \dfrac{1}{\text{capital coefficient}} = \dfrac{1}{2.5}$

$=0.4$ and the annual growth rate$=15/2.5=6$ per cent. The following year's (second year's) national income would therefore become 106.

If we suppose that the increase in consumption were 5 in the second year ($\Delta C_1 = C_1 - C_0 = 5$), then $C_1 = C_0 + \Delta C_1 = 90$, and $I_1 = 16$. Suppose further that β_c in the first year is known to be 0.5, which means that we needed investment of 10 to increase the consumption-goods supply by 5. If so, out of 15 of I_0, 10 must have been invested in the C sector and 5 in the

[3] *Ibid.*, p. 25.

K sector.   Hence $\lambda_c = 2/3$ and $\lambda_k = 1/3$.   Then $\beta_k = \dfrac{16-15}{5}$
$= 0.2$ But what does this mean, that β_k is equal to 0.2? β_k is
a ratio between the increment of investment and that part
of investment which is regarded to have been allocated to the
investment-goods sector.   In other words, what is calculated
here is the increment of "income" presumably generated by
investment in "the investment-goods sector," and "income"
of "the investment-goods sector" is nothing but the increment
of investment itself.   But in order to express the productivity
of capital in each sector by β, which is related to the method
of production, it is necessary to define the production of consumption and investment goods as separate economic activities.
Moreover, investment goods must be non-depreciatory permanent assets.   In practice, however, all this is impossible.
Producers' goods can be used either for the production of
consumption goods or for the production of more producers'
goods.   Therefore, to cite the arithmetic example just discussed,
it is quite possible to increase investment by 21 in the second
year's national income of 106 while keeping consumption
fixed at 85.   In the same way, we can make consumption 91
and hold investment at 15 as in the first year, and so on.   The
fact that these alternatives exist is precisely the circumstance
which gives rise to an *economic* problem.   Therefore the β_k
implied in the Mahalanobis model is essentially different from
the income-coefficient for durable capital goods that could be
estimated statistically, and must also be distinguished from
β_1, β_2, and β_3, which lend themselves to the approximate
estimation of this kind.   The basic difficulty seems to lie in
the partitioning of the economy into sectors by means of
Keynesian net aggregate concepts—a method with many

advantages in developing theoretical models—and then treating each sector as if it were an economic activity unique in some technological sense.

The second point I should like to make about the Mahalanobis model is that the necessary logical relations between its categories are not thoroughly thought out. It seems that this sort of difficulty tends to occur whenever one concentrates on the mathematical implications of one's argument, to the neglect of its realistic meaning in the actual economy or of the intrinsic limitations of the model itself. One must in general be especially cautious on this point in any attempt to apply an abstract model to the growth problem of under-developed countries.

For example, after Mahalanobis defines his β's (productivities of investment) and his θ's (capital-labor ratios) algebraically, he treats them as if they were mutually independent, and then poses a problem: "Let us suppose that the values of all θ's are doubled but β's remain the same,"[4] Let us examine, in terms of Mahalanobis' own definitions, what it means to pose a problem in this manner. If we write out his definitions of terms:

$$\beta = (\Delta Y)/(\lambda K), \ \theta = (\lambda K)/(\Delta L)$$
$$\therefore \quad \beta\theta = (\Delta Y)/(\Delta L)$$

Since θ is assumed to be constant by him, the marginal value $(\Delta Y/\Delta L)$ equals the average value (Y/L). Thus $\beta\theta$ equals the productivity of one worker. In this case, proposing to double the value of θ while keeping β constant means proposing to double the productivity of every worker. This kind of productivity rise is not very easy to achieve, unless there are substantial changes in the economy. Therefore, if he desired

[4] *Ibid.*, p. 43.

to double the value of θ, Mahalanobis should have realized, as an economist, that β should have fallen at least to some extent.

Another example, slightly more complicated, might be given here to show insufficient study of the inter-relationships between categories. The Mahalanobis model does not include any clear relationships between demand and supply. Let us see what happens if we add the condition of equilibrium between the two, namely the equilibrium between the increment of supply and the increment of demand for consumption goods. On the demand side, if we let γ be the marginal propensity to consume, $\Delta C = \gamma \Delta Y$. Since $\Delta Y = \beta K$, and $\gamma = (1-\alpha)$, α being the marginal propensity to save, ΔC becomes:

$$\Delta C \text{ (demand)} = (1-\alpha)\, \beta K$$

On the supply side, on the other hand:

$$\Delta C(\text{supply}) = \lambda_c \beta_c K = \beta_c (1-\lambda_k) K$$

Therefore, if ΔC (demand) $= \Delta C$(supply):

$$(1-\alpha)\beta K = \beta_c (1-\lambda_k) K$$

or:

$$\frac{\beta}{\beta_c} = \frac{1-\lambda_k}{1-\alpha}$$

The condition $\beta/\beta_c = (1-\lambda_k)/(1-\alpha)$ means that if $\beta = \beta_c$, then $\alpha = \lambda_k$. That is to say, the marginal propensity to save must equal the percentage of investment allocated to the K sector.[5] More generally, the condition $\beta/\beta_c = (1-\lambda_k)/(1-\alpha) = \lambda_c/\gamma$ dictates that the ratio of β to β_c must equal the ratio of the percentage of total investment allocated to the C-sector to

[5] It should be noted that this condition is exactly the same as a condition derived from the Feldman model by E.D. Domar. Cf. Domar, *Essays in the Theory of Economic Growth*, (New York: Oxford University Press, 1957), p. 234.

the marginal propensity to consume. In general, Mahalanobis does not consider exhaustively the relations between demand and supply in his model, a reflection of his failing that he did not pursue thoroughly enough the logically necessary interrelations between the categories of his own model.

Now let us examine the Mahalanobis' model from another point of view. Since the β's are constants in his model, their marginal and average values are equal. Therefore the reciprocal of β, or $1/\beta$, represents the additional capital needed to produce a unit of additional income, i.e., the marginal capital coefficient. Then $1/\beta$ is nothing but the technical coefficient for a factor of production, namely "capital." On the other hand, the technical coefficient for another factor of production, "labour," can be expressed as L/Y, since this is the amount of labour needed to generate a unit of additional income. Moreover, as analyzed above, it can be represented by $1/\beta\theta = \Delta L/\Delta Y = L/Y$.

If we calculate, for each of the four sectors (K, C_1, C_2, and C_3), the amounts of capital and labour needed to increase income by one million rupees, the figures in the following table (and the diagram) can be obtained:

Sector	Capital (Rs. Million)	Labour (Man-Years)
K	5.00	250
C_1	2.86	315
C_2	0.86	320
C_3	2.22	593

In general, it is common sense that a sector which needs a large amount of additional capital to produce one unit of additional income should need a smaller amount of additional labour, and vice versa. But our table does not show this to be the case here. For example, in order to generate a million rupees of income, sector C_3 requires more of both capital and labour than sector C_2. This fact, which is more vividly shown in the diagram, tells us clearly that C_3 is an inefficient activity, and makes us suspect that the computed values for the β's and θ's might have been off the mark. If we multiply β by θ in each sector, this gives us the amount of income generated by one worker in each sector. The calculation reveals that the amount of income generated by one worker in the C_2 sector is Rs. 3125, whereas the corresponding amount in the C_3 sector is Rs. 1687. When we consider the fact that the C_3 sector is the service sector (including education and transportation), while the C_2 sector includes agriculture and household industry, it is difficult to

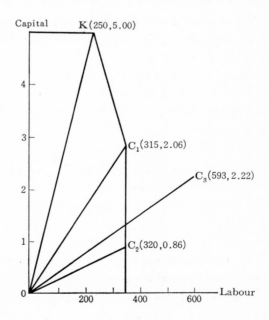

believe that one worker in the latter can generate twice the value of income of that in the former.

If we suppose that "capital" and "labour" are factors of production with technical coefficients as given in the foregoing table (and plotted in the diagram above), the Mahalanobis model can be converted easily into a linear-programming problem.[6] If we represent the technical coefficients of "capital" and "labour" respectively by a's and b's and let (omitting K sector since it is a given condition):

K=Expected supply of "capital"

L=Expected additional employment of "labour"

Y=Target increment of income produced

the problem can be formulated as a linear-programming one of maximizing Y, subject to the conditions:

$$K=a_1Y_1+a_2Y_2+a_3Y_3 \qquad (3.1)$$

$$L=b_1Y_1+b_2Y_2+b_3Y_3 \qquad (3.2)$$

$$Y_1\geqslant0, \; Y_2\geqslant0, \; Y_3\geqslant0 \qquad (3.3)$$

For the Mahalanobis model, equation (3.3) must be replaced by:

$$\bar{Y}=Y_1+Y_2+Y_3 \qquad (3.3)$$

where $\bar{Y}$ is given as Rs. 25.3 billion, as calculated on the assumption of the annual growth rate of income of 5 per cent. But if we try to maximise Y in the linear-programming problem above, the solution will be:

---

[6] For this point, I wish to acknowledge my indebtedness to Professor Ryutaro Komiya of Tokyo University. Cf. Komiya, "A Note on Professor Mahalanobis' Model of Indian Economic Planning," *Review of Economics and Statistics,* February, 1959, pp. 29–35.

Sector	Increase in Employment (Millions)	Investment Allocation (Rs. Million)	Increased Income (Rs. Million)
K	0.9	18,500	3,700
C_1	1.9	16,900	5,910
C_2	8.2	20,000	25,750
C_3	0	0	0
Total	11.0	56,000	35,360

In this solution, the increase in income amounts to Rs. 35.4 billion, as compared to Mahalanobis' Rs. 29.0 billion, an increase of over 20 per cent. As shown above, therefore, if the maximization of income is our sole objective, there is an optimal solution. But as in the case of the Mahalanobis model, if we set a 5 per cent economic growth rate as our target (in addition to various other conditions and parameters), the solution obtained will merely be one of non-contradiction with the given conditions and may easily be quite unstable, as will be shown in the following illustration.

Using Mahalanobis' estimated coefficient (β's and θ's), if we compute the income per worker in the three consumption goods sectors (C_1, C_2, C_3), the results are:

$$C_1......\text{Rs. } 3062$$
$$C_2......\text{Rs. } 3125$$
$$C_3......\text{Rs. } 1687$$

According to the objectives and conditions postulated, the total increment of income is fixed at Rs. 29 billion, of which Rs. 3.7 billion are to be generated in the K sector. Hence, the remaining Rs. 25.3 billion are to be generated from the three C sectors. Furthermore, of the expected total increase in employment of 11 million workers, 900 thousand are to be absorbed by the K sector, leaving the remaining 10.1 million

34

to be added in the three C sectors. If this is the case, the average income generated per worker must be Rs. 2530. The figure cannot deviate from 2530, if the solution is to satisfy the conditions set forth by Mahalanobis. Since the income generated per worker in the C_1 and C_2 sectors is considerably higher than Rs. 2530, the amount generated per worker in the C_3 sector has to be considerably less than Rs. 2530. Considering that θ_3 appears underestimated, if we change it from Rs. 3750 to Rs. 6000, $\beta_3\theta_3$ (income generated per worker in the C_3 sector) becomes Rs. 2700 and no solution can be found, because $\beta_3\theta_3 > 2530$ in this event. In case θ_3 is assumed to be Rs. 5000, $\beta_3\theta_3$ becomes Rs. 2250, and it looks as though there will be a solution, but the solution as regards incremental employment for each sector will be as follows:

$$C_1 \text{ sector} \quad -0.8 \text{ million}$$
$$C_2 \text{ sector} \quad +7.1 \text{ million}$$
$$C_3 \text{ sector} \quad +3.8 \text{ million}$$

This analysis shows how large an influence the coefficients (β's and θ's) have on the solution, and indicates the danger of relying too much on the Mahalanobis type of model in the development planning if the estimated values of the β's and θ's do not correspond closely to the actual ones.

Even disregarding all these matters, there are other reasons why one must exercise caution in using the Mahalanobis model. For example, unless we assume that the situation in the base year is one of optimal equilibrium, we cannot say that the solution obtained from this model is "optimal." Furthermore, it is meaningless to treat the β's and θ's as constants and marginal and average figures as equal, when India's intention is to revolutionize her industrial structure and to introduce substantial innovations in industrial technology. It is in short a dubious procedure to try to solve the Mahalanobis model for the optimal allocation of resources when the problem is the economic growth of an under-developed country faced with all kinds of political and economic problems peculiar to itself.

V

Here we have confined ourselves to the immanent criticism of the Mahalanobis model itself. But of course the relevance of such a model to development problems lies in its role when it is actually applied. Mahalanobis himself did not try to regard the values of his solution as the absolutely optimal ones, but considered many other sociological, political, and economic problems in making his final recommendations to the Government for the Second Five-Year Plan. Thus, when we examine India's Second Five-Year Plan, we observe that there is manifested a strong awareness that the problem of development is in fact many-sided. Nevertheless, it can easily be recognised that the framework of the plan is based upon the solution of the Mahalanobis model, and even though the model's limitations are taken into account, it cannot be denied that no alternative theory of systematic character is indicated in its place.

Since I have written more extensively elsewhere[7] on this subject, here I should like to suggest quite briefly what I consider to be the basic problems in connection with the methods and contents of any development plan:

7) S. Tsuru, *Keizai no Ronri to Genjitsu*, Tokyo, 1959, Part IV, ch. 1.

1. Above all, we must examine most rigorously the socio-economic background of the specific country in question. Then, in connection with the task of "primary accumulation," one should slove the problems of raising investment funds, of the genesis of modern industrial capitalists, and likewise of the genesis of "free" wage-earning labourers.

2. One should make clear the institutional motive force of economic development. If the objective is the achievement of a purely capitalistic system, the motive force will be profit, whereas if it is a socialistic system, it will be the "planning principle." If the objective is to build a mixed economy, the problem of motive force becomes so much harder.

Once one attempts to give rigorous consideration to problems of this kind, it becomes obvious how one-sided is the solution obtained through the Mahalanobis' "optimisation" procedure. Fortunately, the problems of economic development of the under-developed countries are bound to confront the reality, and, in so doing, will objectively reveal any limitations which specific development theories may have. Therefore, the task of casting off unworkable theories could be left to the sifting role of time and history.

*Translator's Appendix**

As an exercise in linear programming, and in carrying out Professor Tsuru's "optimisation" procedures (Section IV) to their logical extreme, we have completed the following chart, which we hope is self-explanatory, by dropping Mahalanobis' assumption that the investment-goods allocation parameter λ_k must be 0.33.

* By M. Bronfenbrenner and C.S. Khang, (University of Minnesota).

Sector	λ_k Fixed				λ_k Variable			
	Mahalanobis		Tsuru		Exactly 11 Million Jobs		At Least 11 Million Jobs	
	ΔN	λ	ΔN	λ	ΔN	λ	ΔN	λ
K	0.9	0.33	0.9	0.33	1.6	0.58	0	0
C_1	1.1	0.17	1.9	0.30	0	0	0	0
C_2	4.7	0.21	8.2	0.37	9.4	0.42	22.4	1.00
C_3	4.3	0.29	0	0	0	0	0	0
Total	11.0	1.00	11.0	1.00	11.0	1.00	22.4	1.00
ΔY	29		35		36		70	

These results are not presented as practical for India; we are quite aware that they are not. They are presented only as indicating further the need (stressed by Tsuru) to impose additional conditions on the Mahalanobis model which will avoid equally ridiculous results when optimisation procedures are applied to it.

Chapter 3

THE EFFECTS OF TECHNOLOGY
ON PRODUCTIVITY

[1962]

Preliminary version of this essay was read at the Vienna Congress of the International Economic Association in September 1962. What follows here is a version submitted for publication in the volume, *Problems in Economic Development*, 1965, edited by E.A.G. Robinson. The volume contains a record of discussion on the paper at the Congress under the chairmanship of Mr. Odd Aukrust. The Japanese version of this essay appeared in *Keizai Kenkyu*, October 1962.

1.   The central theme of this paper is a renewed plea for careful distinction between the real aspect and the value aspect in economic theorizing; and for this purpose it might be better to start the discussion with an example which appears to reflect insufficient awareness of the need for such a distinction.

We are treated with an increasing number of studies which purport to quantify the effects of technology on productivity by separating them from those of capital accumulation.[1]   The

[1] Not intended to be exhaustive, the list of such literature may include: R. Solow, 'Technical Change and the Aggregate Production Function', *The Review of Economics and Statistics*, August 1957; R. Solow, 'Investment and Technical

point I intend to make can be illustrated by any one of them, but here I shall use a modified version of the Johansen's model as a starting point. Seeing that how to measure capital is a knotty problem, he proposed a model which did not require statistical figures for the stocks of capital in the empirical analysis. His model is in terms of industry production function; but I modify it into the aggregate production function.

2. Let the production function be the Cobb-Douglas type

$$Y = AK^{\alpha}L^{1-\alpha} \tag{1}$$

with usual assumptions of constant returns to scale and neutral technological progress. The factor A subsumes shifts in the production function and may be expressed as Ae^{rt}. Dividing both sides of (1) by L and defining $m \equiv \dfrac{Y}{L}$ and $k \equiv \dfrac{K}{L}$, we obtain

$$m = Ae^{rt}k^{\alpha}. \tag{2}$$

From this, we derive a relation

$$g(m) = r + \alpha \cdot g(k) \tag{3}$$

where $g(\ )$ expresses the rate of growth, telling us that the growth rate of labour productivity can be decomposed into the rate of 'technological change' and the growth rate of capital-labour ratio multiplied by the elasticity α. The ratio for which statistical measures have been calculated by Solow, Massell, etc., is $r/g(m)$ which we shall designate as a. Then (3) can be rewritten as

Progress' in *Mathematical Methods in the Social Sciences* 1959, edited by K.J. Arrow, S. Karlin and P. Suppes, 1960; B.F. Massell, 'Capital Formation and Technological Change in United States Manufacturing', *The Review of Economics and Statistics*, May 1960; E.D. Domar, 'On the Measurement of Technological Change', *The Economic Journal*, December 1961; and L. Johansen, 'A Method for Separating the Effects of Capital Accumulation and Shifts in Production Functions upon Growth in Labour Productivity', *The Economic Journal*, December 1961.

$$a = 1 - \alpha \cdot \frac{g(k)}{g(m)} \,. \tag{4}$$

Assuming that the cost minimization principle is carried through with no monopoly power, we obtain the condition

$$\frac{cK}{\alpha} = \frac{wL}{1-\alpha} \tag{5}$$

where c and w are the costs which are associated with the use of one unit of capital and labour, respectively. We may call them the real profit per unit of capital and the wage rate per unit of labour. From (5), we obtain

$$\frac{K}{L} \,(\equiv k) = \frac{\alpha}{1-\alpha} \cdot \frac{w}{c} \tag{6}$$

hence, we derive a relation

$$g(k) = g(w) - g(c) \tag{7}$$

inasmuch as we assume the elasticity α to be constant. Inserting (7) into (4), we obtain

$$a = 1 - \alpha \frac{g(w) - g(c)}{g(m)} \,. \tag{8}$$

Now, since $w = (1-\alpha) \dfrac{Y}{L}$ or $\dfrac{w}{m} = 1 - \alpha$, and α is assumed to be constant, $g(w)$ has to be equal to $g(m)$. Further, if we write $g(c)/g(w) = h$, we can simplify (8) into

$$a = 1 - \alpha + \alpha h \,. \tag{9}$$

Here the expression h is something similar to the reciprocal of Johansen's 'w', or the 'relative increase in wages'. If capital grows at the same rate as output, obviously c has to be constant inasmuch as $\dfrac{K}{Y} = \dfrac{\alpha}{c}$ from the cost-minimization condition.

And in this case $g(c)=0$, simplifying (8) into

$$a=1-\alpha. \tag{10}$$

3.   Let us look at the equation (9) again. α is the relative share of capital which has been known to be fairly stable, in mature countries like the United States, in the vicinity of 0.25. Given this stable parameter α, all that we have to know is the value of h in order to estimate the effects of technology on labour productivity.   And it is Johansen's claim that h can be estimated without concerning us with the precise definition of the capital concept since it is the ratio between the rate of change in the cost per unit of capital and the rate of change in the cost per labour.   *A priori*, this ratio can be inferred to be rather small.

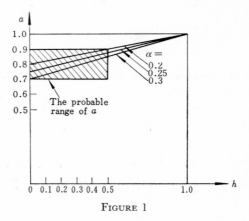

FIGURE 1

Not only in theory, but in the real world also, $g(w)$ tends to be equal to $g(m)$, whereas $g(c)$ or the rate of change of the profit rate is likely to be nearer to zero than to $g(w)$.   Thus we may guess that h in most instances has the value less than 0.5. On the basis of such empirical guesswork we can plot the equation (9) as in Figure 1.   And there it can easily be seen that

42

the range within which *a* can move is fairly restricted, possibly between 0.7 and 0.9.

4. What is the significance of the value of *a* as measured by the use of the equation (9)?

Firstly, apart from theory or substance, the arithmetical fact that the range within which *a* can move is very narrow, lessens, it appears to me, the significance of the result we obtain. Suppose that someone undertakes a laborious task of measuring *a* for a number of countries like the U.K., Germany, France, Italy and Japan using the Solow method for the U.S.A., carefully compiling the statistics to make them comparable and consistent, and obtain the results showing that *a* is equal, let us say, to 80 per cent for the U.K., 78 per cent for Germany, 82 per cent for France, 75 per cent for Italy and 84 per cent for Japan. Can we draw from such an array of figures any significant conclusion as regards the degree of contribution which techonological progress has made, in these countries, to raising the productivity of labour?

Secondly, the restrictive assumptions underlying the equation (9) should be examined more closely. The usual assumptions implied in the aggregate Cobb-Douglas function, as well as the assumption of profit maximization under the competitive condition, are, I believe, not too serious. The biggest problem concerns the matter of units. In order that the Cobb-Douglas function be applicable, both capital and labour have to be identifiable in homogeneous physical units. Let us take the easier case of labour. It is easy enough to count the number of workers engaged and even the number of labour-hours worked. But surely, a Japanese worker of 1870s, with all his dexterity in hands and his common-sense in handling simple tools, would be no equal to his brethren of 1960s in literacy and the knowledge of mechanical equipments of all sorts. If we count the former's one hour's labour as one, we must count the latter's one hour's labour as more than one, just as we would do the similar adjustment in relation to contemporaneous labourers of two different grades. We are yet to see someone perform this seemingly impossible task of reducing the historical series of labour-hours worked to a homogeneous unit.

The case of capital is far more complicated, as has been pointed out by Joan Robinson and others. Johansen's claim that his method can skirt around this difficulty is tenuous, for the rate of profit, or 'the cost associated with the use of capital', is a ratio which, no matter how unambiguous it may be, still presupposes a particular way of measuring the denominator, capital. Between the restrictive concept of capital as a factor consistent with the aggregate Cobb-Douglas function and the concept of capital conventionally used in the calculation of the rate of profit, there is a long series of bridges that have to be crossed; and few of them are easy to cross. Let us postulate, for example, a world in which there is only one kind of machine. 'Ideally what one would like to measure is the annual flow of capital services' (Solow). Now, a machine, like a labourer, has a finite life of its own. So long as it is in active use, it can be assumed to render more or less the same 'quantity' of service every year. But the *value* of a machine, which is relevant to the profit rate calculation, depreciates as it nears the end of its life. One might try to get around this difficulty by taking the gross stock instead of the net stock. But then, a change in the durability of the machine could affect the gross stock magnitude without changing the 'quantity' of current services rendered.[2]

---

[2] On this point, Solow simply says that 'there is nothing to be done about this.' (*Op. cit.*, *The Review of Economics and Statistics*, p. 314).

Secondly, a machine, like a labourer, can be improved in its performance capacity through technological progress without any change in durability or in a number of labour-hours required to produce it. Should not such a machine be counted, in the Cobb-Douglas function, as a multiple of the simple machine? Here is a problem quite similar to the case of the labour factor mentioned earlier. Thirdly, compare two machines exactly alike in all respects (including their durability and age) except that one is drawn from an economy with a higher product-wage rate. As Joan Robinson pointed out, 'the value of the two machines is different, and the investment required to create them is different. A difference in value remains if we deflate them by the wage rate, for in two economies with different product-wage rates the rate of profit and therefore the rate of interest are different.'[3] Furthermore, the real world makes use of a thousand and one different types of machines, both substitutive and complementary. A formidable index number problem arises here. In addition, the concept of capital that is relevant to the profit calculation subsumes not only fixed capital but also working capital. Some economists would, even now as in the classical era, prefer to include what Marx called 'variable capital' (wages payment in advance of the sale of products) as a part of capital.

In other words, capital is essentially a value concept; and one cannot escape from its value implication as affected by the rate of interest, the time pattern of wage rate changes, etc., unless we assume a radically simplified economy of one-type machine with no technological change.

Now, suppose we close our eyes to all the knotty problems

[3] Joan Robinson, 'The Production Function and the Theory of Capital—A Reply', *The Review of Economic Studies*, No. 62, p. 247.

in crossing a series of bridges which extend across the aggregate Cobb-Douglas function and the real world and look at the equation (9) without specifying the significance of *a*. Call it, for example, simply the '*a*-ratio'. Both α and *h*, i.e., the capital's share and the relative growth rate of the profit rate with respect to the wage rate, are empirically observable magnitudes. The *a*-ratio can be derived for any economy in which α is measured to be fairly stable over a span of years and the reasonably accurate statistics of the profit rate and the wage rate are available. We refrain from identifying the *a*-ratio with the degree of contribution which technological progress makes to raising the productivity of labour; but could we not at least say that it measures some kind of *real* (as contrasted to *value*) contribution of a certain occurrence to some kind of *real* (as contrasted to *value*) increase in products? *A priori*, we are not prevented from answering this question in the affirmative. The *a*-ratio is in the world of *real* magnitudes and α and *h* are in the world of *value* magnitudes; and the equation (9) tells us that the former is determined by the latter. Such a relation or its inverse is not at all unusual in the neo-classical theorizing as is exemplified by the equating of the marginal physical product of labour with the wage rate under the competitive condition. We have been quite accustomed to the theorizing of this type that most of us do not even suspect that here lurks a methodological problem which becomes peculiarly relevant in connection with certain types of problems. Before going any further, we can at lesat say that the *a*-ratio as determined by the equation (9) is, though intended to be *real* in its content, highly dependent on the workings of the type of economic system to which α and *h* are inseparably related. In other words, it is conceivable that with the same technological progress

46

a socialist economy will be characterized by the a-ratio different in magnitude from that in a capitalist economy. It is for this reason that I propose to trace, in what follows, somewhat elementary steps in the discussion of technological progress with a view to distinguishing the real aspect and the value aspect.

5. The economist who showed the keenest awareness of the need for distinguishing the value aspect from the real (or physical) aspect was, I believe, Marx.[4] But it is not necessary to dwell upon his systematic discussion of this problem in order to realize what is involved here. Economists like Keynes and Harrod, who performed a pioneering role in the development of modern macro-economic theory, were, in their own way, aware of the peculiar difficulty which presented itself in the matter of the choice of units—the difficulty which stemmed from the double character (the value and the physical) of the production process, especially of the economic system as a whole. In criticizing Pigou's method of arriving at the net national dividend by deducting 'normal' obsolescence, Keynes made a revealing comment: 'Since this deduction is not a deduction

---

[4] See, in particular, chapter 7 of volume I of *Capital*, entitled: 'The Labor-Process, and the Process of Producing Surplus-Value'. (In the German edition, currently available, this is chapter 5.) It was natural for Marx to insist upon such a distinction since he was concerned especially with the analysis of the *peculiarly capitalistic character* of the social relations of production. Cf., for example, 'The labor-process......is human action with a view to the production of use-values, appropriation of natural substances to human requirements; it is the necessary condition for effecting exchange of matter between man and Nature; it is the everlasting Nature-imposed condition of human existence, and therefore is independent of every social phase of the existence, or rather, is common to every such phase.......As the taste of the porridge does not tell you who grew the oats, no more does this simple process tell you of itself what are the social conditions under which it is taking place, whether under the slave-owner's brutal lash, or the anxious eye of the capitalist, whether Cincinnatus carries it on in tilling his modest farm or a savage in killing wild animals with stones.' (*Capital*. vol. I, Foreign Languages Publishing House, Moscow, pp. 183–4.)

in terms of money, he is involved in assuming that there can be a change in physical quantity, although there has been no physical change; i.e. he is covertly introducing changes in *value*'.[5]   Keynes' solution was, as is well known, to adopt the labour-unit and/or the wage-unit 'by taking an hour's employment of ordinary labour as our unit and weighing an hour's employment of special labour in proportion to its remuneration'.[6]   This is an approach remarkably close to that of Marx, except that in the latter's case 'ordinary labour' as the unit is visualized to change its quality historically.

Harrod, too, wrestled with a similar problem when he posed the problem of whether neutral technical progress required new investment and answered that it was a question of definition—that the answer depended on whether a labour standard of value is chosen or a goods standard of value.   His preference was for the latter for a number of reasons which we shall not go into here.[3]

The distinction between a labour standard and a goods standard corresponds to that of the value aspect and the physical aspect.   Whereas micro-economics for a capitalist society can navigate almost entirely in the world of values, macro-economics, especially of the dynamic type, finds it difficult to dissociate itself from the real or physical aspect of its subject matter.   In this sense, the fact that Keynes, who was interested more in the short-run problem with no technological change, chose a labour standard and Harrod, who was concerned with a dynamic economics, chose a goods standard is easily understandable.

[5] Italics in original. J.M. Keynes, *The General Theory of Employment, Interest and Money*, pp. 38–9.
[6] *Ibid.*, p. 41.
[7] See R. Harrod, *Towards a Dynamic Economics*, pp. 28–34.

Having said this, I must add immediately that problems in dynamic macro-economics, so long as it is intended to be economics, cannot avoid navigating in the world of values also, and that our task is a peculiarly difficult one of combining the two aspects in an appropriate manner.

6. The real or physical aspect of production can only be described and does not easily render itself to abstract analysis. Whatever the type of economic system a society may have, the process of production in the society as a whole involves the exertion of efforts by all kinds of men, with differing qualifications, who operate upon nature with objects fashioned out of nature in the circumstance of natural endowment and social environment not necessarily uniform everywhere. Operating workers, at any point of time, may be endowed with heritage, both technical and cultural, which is the accumulation passed on from their forefathers. Those selected few who are in the position of making decisions for a producing unit may have an aggressive outlook conditioned by the social milieu or by their innate propensity, and again they may not have it. Language is no less a factor in the situation, as can easily be surmised from the comparison of the three countries: Japan with the phoneticized media, China with innumerable characters requiring years to master, and India with multi-lingual heritage not adapted yet to modern science and technology. It should be mentioned, moreover, that the problem of material balance in terms of use-values is quite relevant to the real or physical aspect of production.

Once we turn to the value aspect of production we cannot escape, in our discussion, from the framework of a particular economic system in which production is carried on. In general terms we could say that the value aspect of production would have the following components, all expressed in the same unit so that the addition is feasible:

$$
\begin{bmatrix} \text{Cost of raw} \\ \text{materials} \\ \text{and fuel} \end{bmatrix} + \begin{bmatrix} \text{Replace-} \\ \text{ment cost} \end{bmatrix} + \begin{bmatrix} \text{Value} \\ \text{added} \end{bmatrix}
$$

But how this unit comes about is dependent on the mode of production (as, for example, the competitive pricing in a private enterprise economy or the accounting pricing in a centrally planned economy) and how the value-added component is distributed among various categories is certainly not independent of the class relations of the society. In a feudal society, for example, the ruling class could claim a sizable portion of the value added on the basis of their *status* without in any way participating in the production process. In a capitalist society, at least in theory, knowledge as such does not receive its own marginal product, although few will doubt the substantial contribution it makes in the real or physical aspect of production. In a centrally planned economy it is perfectly possible deliberately to calculate the *value* reward for 'knowledge' in approximate accord with its obvious contribution in the real aspect. Again, the rentier income, as Keynes observed, may well be a historically transient category even within the framework of capitalism. Capitalism may well be a most efficient economic system; but to admit this does not absolve us from recognizing the efficacy of specific value relations which characterize different modes of production.

7. Technological progress, too, has its real and value aspects. Whether it takes place in the Soviet Union or in the United States, its real aspect can be described in almost exactly the same way. How to describe it, probably, would be the task of an engineer who would have to focus upon multiple causal relations

in which the development of basic science, quality of labour, specific resources endowment, etc., would all have to be brought in. Essentially, the nature of this task is a description which ends up with a demonstration that the ratio between the physical output and the labour (both direct and indirect) input has risen —the ratio which we usually call 'the productivity of labour.' In such discussion of the real aspect it is not necessary that the unit of labour shall be in terms of the abstract concept of historically unchanging simple labour. In fact, it is generally understood that here labour is in terms of the biological unit which commonly changes its quality over time. Focussing our attention to this ratio, we can pose an inquiry as to relative contributions of various *real* factors to the rise of the ratio. A number of factors which are relevant may be enumerated:

A. Education and training which enhance the quality of labour.

B. Public health and medical services in general which contribute towards maintaining the continual effective performance of operating workers.

C. Cultural amenities which have the function of raising the morale of workers.

D. Industrial harmony which can elicit a greater degree of cooperation from the working class than the lack of it.

E. The improvement in the media of communications, including the modernization of language.

F. Social and political tensions of constructive character, including what Rostow called 'reactive nationalism.'

G. Social innovations in the sense of 'new methods of inducing human beings to compete and cooperate in the social progress' (Kuznets).

H. Technological innovations of both 'proper' and 'derived' types.[8]

I. The mere increase in the scale of production entirely apart from any technological change.

It is hard to deny that each one of these factors, in varying degrees in different historical circumstances, has been relevant to the raising of labour productivity; and it is probably harder to assign quantitative weights to them in a given situation.

In the Japan of the last quarter of the nineteenth century, when she is said to have accomplished the Rostovian 'take off' with a remarkable speed, the factors like (A), (E) and (F) above were undoubtedly of major importance, making it possible to achieve the 5 to 4 per cent annual growth rate with the net investment ratio of less than 10 per cent. A value relation like the capital-output ratio is bound to reflect such specific circumstances of the country in the real aspect. And so long as we confine our attention to the real aspect, it is not very meaningful to ask what percentage in the rise of labour productivity was due to technological innovations and the remainder due to the increase in the 'quantity of capital' per worker.

8. If we limit ourselves to quantifiable magnitudes, it is, of course, not impossible to set up a model through which we might indicate certain logical relations implied in technological progress as viewed from the real aspect.

Assume an economy which produces corn only with the aid of tractors which, however, can be improved upon. Let us assume that the total quantity of corn (Q) to be produced remains constant, as well as the total number of tractors (K) in operation

<hr>

[8] Cf. Charles Kennedy, 'Technical Progress and Investment', *The Economic Journal*, June 1961, p. 294.

at any time.   Tractors are replaced as they wear out, and the number of them replaced each year (D) is, of course, determined by the durability (n), or

$$\overline{K}=nD .$$

The number of workers engaged in the production of tractors (L_i) is determined by their physical productivity (m_i), or

$$D=m_iL_i .$$

The number of workers in the sector of corn production (L_c) is, we assume, uniquely determined by the number (a) needed to operate each one of the tractors, or,

$$L_c=a\overline{K}$$

and their productivity (m_c) can be related to Q as follows:

$$\overline{Q}=m_cL_c .$$

It is clear that m_c cannot be independent of a, nor is it independent of m_i if the latter falls to make the tractor bigger and better. Defining

$$L\equiv L_i+L_c$$

we can express, on the basis of the above relations, the social productivity $Q/L(\equiv m)$ as

$$m=\frac{anm_im_c}{1+anm_i} .$$

In such an economy, the nature of technological progress in the broad sense can be of the following types:

(1) a declines, or the number of workers in the corn sector needed to operate the given tractor can be economized due to, say, an improvement in the technical qualification of the corn sector workers.   In this case, it might be assumed that m_c rises exactly to offset the decline in a.   Then, obviously, the numera-

tor remains constant while the denominator falls, thus raising the value of m.

(2) n rises, or the durability of tractors is lengthened without any change in other variable.   In this case, too, m rises as a result.

(3) m_i rises, or an innovation takes place in the tractor producing sector without any change in the type of tractors made.   Again, m rises as a result.

(4) m_i falls but m_c rises more, so that the product $m_i m_c$ is bigger than before, or a new and bigger type of tractor is introduced with no change in a or n.   Upshot will be the rise in m as in other cases.

The model of this type is essentially physical and makes no mention of the wage level or of the 'quantity of capital'.   However, it is possible, within the limitation of the real aspect, to refine the model further by introducing both.   If we write w for the real wage rate in terms of corn and v for the wage-value of a tractor, we can say

$$v = \frac{w}{m_i}$$

since the number of workers required to produce one tractor is $1/m_i$.   Further, the total number of tractors in existence, K, can be expressed as

$$K = \frac{1}{a} L_c .$$

Thus the wage cost of the *gross* stock of tractors is

$$vK = \frac{w}{am_i} L_c .$$

Dividing this by output of $Q(=m_c L_c)$, we obtain a ratio which we might call the 'capital-output ratio', written as

$$\frac{w}{am_i m_c} \; .$$

This, incidentally, is an expression for the 'capital-output ratio' which could be derived from a model different from ours here.[9] It implies that the ratio can remain constant even if productivities change so long as the real wage rate rises *pari passu* with $am_i m_c$. Various other abstract relations could be derived with the aid of a model like this. But it is essential to remember that its applicability is limited to a type of situation where value relations in the Marxian sense of the term can be entirely abstracted.

9. Once we move to the value aspect of technological progress, we enter the world which, no matter how abstract, cannot escape from the efficacy of a particular mode of production. The concept 'capital', for example, now acquires an institutional dimension. Under capitalism, 'capital' is the basic unit of economic activities guided by the principle of maximizing the return to itself. Thus the return to 'capital' is an institutional category and as such it constitutes an essential component in the process of price formation. Technological progress, as viewed in this world of value relations, is inevitably related to this process of price formation; and it is characteristic under capitalism that innovations are introduced by a private entrepreneur, a category of men who are in the driver's seat, so to speak, who receive special reward for their successful introduction during a limited duration of time before they are generally imitated. Once a specific innovation becomes prevalent, the special reward disappears and competition forces the relevant price to go down. It is possible to discuss in detail, by the

[9] Cf. S. Tsuru, 'A Note on Capital-Output Ratio', *Keizai Kenkyu*, April 1956.

method of comparative statics, how prices may change as a result of this or that type of technological progress which we enumerated in the previous sectoin.

What is especially important in the dynamic value aspect of technological progress, however, is the special reward which accrues to pioneering entrepreneurs; and it is perfectly conceivable that under another mode of production such a reward takes a noneconomic form for the manager of a firm while monetary rewards are given more directly to scientists and engineers.[10] In other words, the question like 'How are the fruits of technological progress distributed between capital and labour?' cannot be answered independently of a particular mode of production in which it takes place. This is the reason why we cast serious doubt, in Part I, on the method of estimating the effect of technological progress, as distinguished from that of capital accumulation, on raising the productivity of labour— the method which essentially depended on the relative share of of a factor in the value aspect of production.

[10] A 'social innovation', as defined by Kuznets in our earlier section, makes this possible.

Chapter 4

MERITS AND DEMERITS OF THE MIXED
ECONOMY IN ECONOMIC DEVELOPMENT
——LESSONS FROM INDIA'S EXPERIENCE——

[1961]

This essay was completed in March 1961 while the author was serving as visiting professor at the University of Rochester and was included in the Volume I of *Studies on Developing Countries: Planning and Economic Development*, published in 1964 by Polish Scientific Publishers. Before publication it was read and submitted for discussion at the annual meeting of the Association of Asian Studies in the spring of 1961.

Introductory

What I propose to do in this paper is firstly to make a somewhat analytical attempt to confront a general case of the mixed economy with certain specified tasks of resources expansion and allocation, and then secondly to turn around, so to speak, to put myself in the position of a policy maker in the newly developing countries of today and ask the question as to what the basic requirements are for their task of economic development. India's experience is relevant especially to the first part and thus is woven into the discussion at a number of points. The second part applies to most of the underdeveloped countries today and is intended more as a supplement for this paper to indicate a broader frame of reference which I believe to be useful for drawing lessons from the experience of any one of them for future policy purposes.

The Nature of the Mixed Economy

The term "mixed economy" is usually used in a generic sense applicable both to an advanced capitalist economy and to an underdeveloped one, and its defining characteristics may be set down as follows:

(1) It is essentially a capitalistic economy; thus the private sector operating with the motive force of profit extends over a major portion of the economy.

(2) The role of the government is recognized to be positive; and not only is the governmental interference with the free play of market mechanism tolerated (or deemed desirable at times), but the operation of a significant sector of the economy under government control and/or ownership is also considered warranted.

(3) There is generally a strong welfare orientation and also the negative attitude on coercion of any kind.

(4) The state is not identified with the interest of any particular class; and thus there operate countervailing powers of various interest groups.

Although such a characterization may fit both India of today and the U.S.A. of the New Deal period, it is obvious that the "mixed economy" of an advanced capitalist country is different from the "mixed economy" of a newly developing country. The degree of development in the institutional aspects of capitalism is different, and thus the problems faced are naturally of different types. In particular, as is envisaged by the Indian government, her "mixed economy" of today could be a stage in the evolutionary process of developing India into "a socialistic pattern of society". In other words, it appears to be best to regard the "mixed economy" not as a distinct mode of production or economic system but as a phase in the life cycle of a certain mode of production. In India's case, the phase may be transitional to socialism and again may not be so. Whichever the case it may be, her present condition as that of the "mixed economy" is quite real; and our problem is to draw lessons from the actual confrontation of a mixed economy with the task of economic development.

The Frame of Reference

With a view to assessing merits and demerits of the mixed economy in general in the tasks of achieving the take-off,[1] I propose here a frame of reference which will enable us to make comparison easier with other modes of production in developmental performance.

The problem of economic development may be visualized in terms of (A) resources expansion and (B) resources allocation. "Resources" in this context consist of (1) manpower and (2) capital.[2] "Manpower" is to be understood here in

[1] The term "take-off" is used here for convenience without necessarily implying agreement with Dr. W.W. Rostow's stages theory of growth.

[2] It is customary to think of naturally endowed physical objects, such as land, mineral deposits, etc., as an important element of "resources". But I believe that

the broad sense of the term to cover not merely the physical existence of a certain number of labour force but also the intensity with which people are willing to exert themselves and also to include what Adam Smith called "acquired and useful abilities of the inhabitants" which of course can be improved through education and training. "Capital" is a much-abused term; and I prefer to avoid using it if I can. But for convenience' sake I compromise and here make it mean both the accumulated physical assets, inclusive of inventories and social overhead structures, and the still uncommitted investible funds. If we interpret the whole of current output as potential capital and thus a part of "resources" under our definition, we may say that the problem of resources allocation partakes the character of resources expansion. Thus resources allocation as regards capital may be discussed in three stages: (a) the aggregative level of $Y=C+I$, giving rise to the problem of determining the ratio of investment to net national product; (b) the sector level, involving the problem of what is often called "allocation parameters"; and (c) the firm level, where the choice of alternative investment plans becomes a relevant issue.

The Mixed Economy Contrasted with Other Systems

With the aid of the frame of reference proposed above, we may now examine the characteristic manner in which the mixed economy solves problems which arise in connection with the expansion and allocation of resources. Contrasting observations on capitalism and socialism will be added as we go along.

Manpower. Usually, underdeveloped countries, whatever such naturally endowed resources can, and had better be, expressed in terms of input flows of manpower and capital with appropriate productivity contents.

the type of economy they may have, do not face the need of expanding the labour force as such.   Often their problem is the
opposite one.   In India's case, for example, the original "Plan-
Frame" by Professor Mahalanobis set the target of creating
11 millions new jobs for the Second Five-Year Plan period.
The target was scaled down to 9.5 millions (7.9 outside agriculture and 1.6 in agriculture) in the actual Plan; and it was
further marked down when the public outlay in the Plan was
reduced.   Actual achievement during the first three years of
the Plan has been the creation of 3.5 millions new jobs outside
agriculture.[3)]   Thus it seems quite clear that India's problem
today is that of creating new jobs and not that of expanding
the number of labour force as such.

Does this imply that another aspect of expanding "manpower" in the broad sense, namely the lifting of the morale of
work force to a higher pitch of exertion, is not called for in
such circumstance and that if it does come about it will aggra-
vate the employment problem as a whole?   Not necessarily.
For the matter of élan is an imponderable factor in society
which could raise productivities all around expanding the surplus which is after all the basis for a higher rate of growth and
more job opportunities.   India's performance in this regard
seems to leave much to be desired.   What this failing is due
to, of course, is a complex problem.   But it appears to me at
least pertinent in this connection to examine consequences of
the mixed economy approach, which India has adopted, especially in contrast to the case of an underdeveloped economy
which has gone through a social revolution.   Even Japan of

[3)] Contrast this achievement to a forecast that "four to five millions new jobs
annually must be created" during the Third Five-Year Plan Period. (See T.
Balogh: 'India's Plan for Survival', *New Statesman*, 24 February 1961, p. 289.)

1868, in a sense, went through such a revolution; and aided partly by what Rostow calls "reactive nationalism", Japan appears to have succeeded in mobilizing the maximum efforts of people in the task of development in the last quarter of the 19th century. The mixed economy of today, on the other hand, tends to favour compromise over the issues of clashing class interests and rather to encourage the exercise of countervailing powers without being able to take a drastic action in either direction to make a particular class supreme; and thus unidirectional élan seems to get lost in the process.

The manpower allocation problem under the mixed economy is essentially solved through the market mechanism as under capitalism. Features peculiar to the mixed economy in this connection may be said to be (1) the attempt to maintain, by governmental action, the social minimum wage and to make it keep pace with the rise in the average productivity of the economy; (2) the generally protective attitude by the government in favour of what are considered to be legitimate demands by trade unions; and (3) active efforts by governments on all levels to facilitate the mobility of labor through the establishment of employment agencies as well as the building of related social overhead structures such as the water and sewage system, etc.

The first two points above are admittedly in the nature of an interference with the untrammeled working of a free competitive system, whereas the third might be considered consistent with it if it does not go too far. Actually the second and the third may conflict with each other over the problem of labour mobility. The reason why they may do so can be traced to the basic character of the mixed economy itself; namely, that the governmental interventions under the mixed economy, welfare-oriented as they may be, are essentially pluralistic and are not organized into a monistic hierarchy of values. If a trade union objects, as it did in India in 1955, to the introduction of automatic power looms on the ground of possible displacement of some of its members, a mixed economy government is constrained to respect the welfare consideration of that particular union on a par with other values in a pluralistic array. The nature of solution is almost always a compromise. Allocation through the free market mechanism has its theoretical defense as regards its optimal performance, and allocation through the centralized planning, when practical, also has its unique advantages. But allocation of manpower under the mixed economy is yet to find a way of combining the merits of the two systems in actual practice.

That the basic principle of manpower allocation is the reliance on the market mechanism implies that monetary inducements play an extremely important role. In fact, a theorem in theoretical economics to the effect that under perfect competition marginal product of labour becomes equal to the wage rate does have a meaning here. To the extent that a particular person contributes to the enlargement of national product, he is rewarded accordingly; and the extent of his contribution is determined by impersonal forces of the market. In the actual world, of course, qualifications of all kinds will enter; and the theorem can only be approximated. But what are we to say as regards the efficacy of such an allocation mechanism if the economy in question has chosen to tolerate, as in India, the earning differential as high as 100 to 1 between the salary of a high government officeal and the *per capita* income of the nation as a whole?[4] This is not merely a rhetoric question, for the

[4] In the United States, such a ratio is about 8 to 1; and in Japan it is about 10 to 1 at present.

sector of government service is not subject to market valuation and furthermore the pay scale of civil servants in higher eche lons in India stands almost at the top of the ladder in the size distribution of income. The relatively high differential which ranking officials enjoy *does* have a desirable effect of inducing competent men of integrity to enter the civil service; but when the differential is too large relative to the average income of the nation, it will also have undesirable effects of distorting and/or diluting the inducement mechanism. For example, universities would find it difficult to recruit the best qualified persons into teaching posts and the standard of higher education would suffer. Again, private corporations, whose revenues depend on market valuation, would feel constrained to pay to employees with technical or managerial competence at a salary-scale which would be out of proportion with the prevailing wage rate, thus perpetuating the condition of extreme inequality of income with its attendant mal-effects on the morale of the working people. It would seem that the present condition in India calls for a general raising, as well as making steeper, of the progressive income tax rates if only for the purpose of bringing about a more rational allocation of manpower.

Capital. As has been mentioned earlier, the expansion of capital resources essentially reduces itself to the problem of allocation of aggregative current output. Loans and grants from abroad constitute, of course, an important way of expanding the resource; and a society with the mixed economy, to the extent it tends to be neutralist in the present context of the world situation, may enjoy an advantage over a clearly-committed one in obtaining such loans and grants at favourable terms from both camps. But in a narrower purview of economic analysis, this aspect of the problem should probably be set aside and we had better concentrate on allocation problems.

Schematically, the problem of allocation in a capitalist society may be represented by the following diagram:

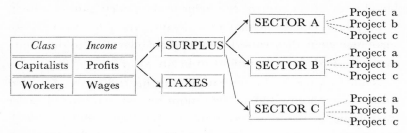

Allocation: (a) in aggregates, (b) by sectors, (c) between projects.

It is characteristic of capitalism to pay out the total of net value added to respective factors of production.   And in this process "wages" stand in an antagonistic position to "profits". How much surplus can be extracted from the economy depends in the first instance, given its productivity level, upon this antagonistic relation.   To the extent that the welfare orientation of mixed economy favours the wage-income, to that extent is the major source of the surplus made smaller.   If it is objected that so long as the level of national income remains the same the rate of saving can be postulated to be the same, I would counter by pointing out that the profit-income under capitalism is by its very nature destined to investment whereas the wages-income, especially in a newly developing country, needs strenuous coaxing in making it resist consumption spending.

Under the economy characterized by centralized planning, on the other hand, the total of net value added need not be distributed.   Theoretically, the surplus is visualized as the fruit of collective action in a society of extensive division of labour— the fruit which defies imputation to specific individuals and/or

65

firms. Thus the surplus can be directly syphoned away to the state in the form, for example, of turnover taxes before distribution takes place. Appropriate use of price control combined with wages control can achieve the policy objective here. It may be pointed out that it is always harder to make people surrender what they consider to be their own than to distribute to them the deducted amount to begin with.

While in a planned economy the surplus is directly extracted from the economy and its size more or less determined by *ex ante* planning, the allocation under capitalism is done through the market mechanism via parametric function of the interest rate. In fact, the rate of interest is the crucial parameter there, not only at the level of allocation of aggregates, but also at the levels where sector allocation is made and the choice among alternative projects is decided. The mixed economy may be said to differ from the case of pure capitalism in two respects; namely:

(a) Inasmuch as the role of the state is substantial under the mixed economy, a part of the surplus usually comes into the hands of the government. The way this is done is either by imposing taxes on the private sector or by making the public sector yield up some surplus. To the extent that direct taxes play a part here, there arises another situation of antagonism, namely, between profits and taxes. In an economy where private profits constitute a major motivating force of economic activities, direct tax on profits cannot but be a dampening factor. The greater the role which it is felt that state is to play, the greater is likely to be the encroachment by the state on the sacred playground, as it were, of private capital; and such a conflict of the two institutional motive forces which basically differ from each other tends to weaken both.

(b) Allocation of the surplus among sectors, under the mixed economy, could be done partly through a more direct means than under capitalism. The use of allocation parameters (λ's) in the Professor Mahalanobis's Plan-Frame for the Second Five-Year Plan is an example of this. Presumably the mixed economy state is capable of using its governmental powers as well as proceeds of the public sector to influence fairly effectively the flow of investment funds to different sectors. However, whether or not the Mahalanobis type of model can provide us with the framework adequate for the purpose is, of course, a separate problem. The "net-sectoring"[5] which he employs renders it very difficult to interpret the empirical meaning of the allocation parameter of the "investment sector" or, for that matter, of the investment productivity of the "investment sector".[6] In any case, it is questionable if the solution he obtained through his model yielded him "an optimum allocation of resources in relation to the basic objectives", as he claims. Such a critique, of course, has nothing to do with the case for or against the allocation performance of a mixed economy.

On the problem of allocation between alternative projects within an industry, a planned economy can also use a "capitalistic" yardstick of the rate of interest. Soviet Union does so in the guise of the "coefficient of effectiveness", although there different "coefficients" are handed down to respective industries by the state. Thus an element of arbitrariness enters in here. But even in abstract theory it may be questioned if

[5] A method of dividing economic activities *only* in terms of final products such as consumption goods purchased by final purchasers, net investment whether in the form of an increase in the stock of fixed capital goods or of net increase in inventories, and so on.

[6] See S. Tsuru: 'Some theoretical doubts on India's Plan-Frame, *Economic Weekly*' (Bombay), Annual Number, January 1957, 77–9.

a unitary yardstick to cover all types of projects (including, of course, projects involving social overhead structures) is conducive to most rational allocation. It is well known that people who do the discounting are often very short-sighted, and also it may be pointed out that uncertainties under capitalism are frequently due to the peculiar institutional characteristics of the system itself. In actual fact, even a capitalist society resorts to a state-directed policy of differential interest rates with good reason. Undeniably, the mixed economy can do the same, and probably more effectively if the whatever extent of planning it does is coordinated rationally with this aspect of the allocation problem.

Limitations of the Mixed Economy

I am aware that the problem of economic development covers a much broader scope than our somewhat restricted discussion, above, in terms of the frame of reference proposed earlier. In fact, the mixed economy may claim its merits in non-economic spheres, such as the matter of individual freedom, of political gradualism, etc. If it happens that a nation in question holds these values especially dear, that nation may be perfectly willing to sacrifice for them the speed of economic growth as such. A simple analogy can be drawn from experience of an individual. A person may value the leisure so much that he is willing to forego the chance of earning more through longer working hours. Just as what can be bought by money is not the only source of personal satisfaction, that which enters into the economists' calculation of national income is not the only object of nation's aspirations. *Generally speaking*, therefore, a mixed-economy nation need not necessarily feel frustrated or "beaten" when it finds itself falling behind central-ly-planned economies in the rate of economic growth. Whether in a concrete case of India the compensating values are in fact sufficiently large is, of course, a separate problem.

If, however, our concern is over the rapid rate of economic growth, our analysis can start, I believe, profitably with the framework I proposed in terms of resources expansion and allo-cation; and limitations of the mixed economy in this regard seem to be fairly clear.

I would attribute the basic cause of these limitations to *the mixture of institutional motive forces*. The mixed economy is es-sentially a capitalist economy. Growth is a built-in charac-teristic of capitalism. It performs best, at least in its hey day, when the system is unfettered by extraneous forces. The state then represents interests of the leading class (i.e. there is an identification of interests between the political power and the economic power), and it restricts its function to matters of law and order. Capitalism is capable of raising welfare of the working class, but it does so only when it does not conflict with the overriding interests of capital. There is no room for doubt which is the master here. In the antagonistic relation between profits and wages, profits cannot lose and in fact do not lose. For the instant profits lose a battle to wages, the capital concern-ed disqualifies itself as a functioning capital. As a matter of fact, profits constitute a source of, as well as an index of con-tribution to, economic growth under capitalism. Now what the mixed economy does is to blunt the pioneering function of private capital by encroaching upon its domain either (a) through coming to the aid of "wages" against "profits", or (b) through taxing profits heavily, or (c) through narrowing the scope within which private capital can operate. Since the

69

basic structure of the economy is still class-oriented without permitting the state to have complete identity of interests with any particular class, the solution to problems arising out of such encroachment essentially partakes the character of compromise. Compromise weakens the growth-oriented ardour of private capital; and this setback is not compensated for by the increased sense of mastery over its fate by the working class. It cannot be denied that paid-out wages have a much higher propensity to consume than profits.[7] Thus, other things being equal, a shift to wages means a slower rate of growth when effective demand is not a limitational element in the situation.

If the level of real wages is very low, as in most underdeveloped countries of today, it is evident that the basic condition of rapid growth is that the rate of increase of real wage should not be as high as the rate of increase of labour productivity. This condition was automatically achieved in the early developmental phase of capitalism. Under the mixed economy it is difficult to resist the parallel movement of the two rates of increase. Thus a need for a special austerity program if rapid economic growth is to be achieved. To what extent India under the two Five-Year Plans succeeded in sparking this realization is not clear to me. But on theoretical grounds, as explained above, I have a suspicion that the intention of Indian leaders in this regard has been thwarted by a formidable barrier of institutional character.

The mixture of institutional motive forces under the mixed

[7] Capitalism is an economy of "free for all". Thus trade unions under capitalism might well say: "If 'free for all', let us fight for our share; but once we are in power, let us be stingy about consuming the pie because the part we save will enable us to enlarge the size of the pie next year". Austerity program may be fought hard by trade unions under capitalism and yet may be willingly adopted by them when the power shifts. There is no contradiction here.

economy is reflected further in the idea of balanced growth. Centrally planned economies operate with a certain degree of ruthlessness in carrying out a program of crude priorities where a number of industries, especially in the sector of producers' goods, are pushed to the maximum often without regard to rational cost. And thus they may succeed in achieving the "break through". Capitalism, on the other hand, makes progress characteristically by "overshooting the mark". Overproduction and surplus capacity constitute a way of progress. They create incentives for the deliberate expansion of market and provide occasions for the liquidation of the least efficient. In part, business cycles are nothing but the pulsation of a vigorous capitalism. The mixed economy, however, is, by its nature, wary of going to either extreme. As is exemplified by Professor Mahalanobis' Plan-Frame for the Second Five-Year Plan, it maps out a framework of balanced growth and targets for various industries come out as a solution consistent with a certain aggregative balance. Such a frame could be achieved if planning principles are carried out to the end. Since the mixed economy does not do so, varied degrees of shortfall can easily ensue. If a shortfall here is compensated by an overachievement there, we may say that the overall aggregate goal is achieved. But the very existence of a plan-frame, to the extent it is effective, is a dampening influence on private capital which thrives best in the atmosphere of unfettered freedom. And furthermore, even if an overachievement is in fact registered, the mixed economy's orientation for balanced growth tends to frown upon it. The net result of all this is that a sector which lags for whatever reason tends to have a dragging influence upon related sectors, thus weakening the growth potential of entire economy,

The mixed edonomy does not necessarily have to favour a closed economy. But since foreign trade is subject to unpredictable and often uncontrollable forces outside the country and also because the nurturing of infant industries seems to come naturally with the ideology of the mixed economy, it tends to favour the development of major industries at home in an early stage of the transition to the take-off. That the international climate today is not so favourable as in the 19th century to the strict free policy of a newly developing country is also a factor in the situation. Thus, as we observe in the case of India, policy measures tend to restrict the area of its economy exposed to international competition. To this extent, India denies to herself the benefit of the international division of labour in the course of her economic development.

Economic Development in Broader Perspective

Thus far I have deliberately restricted my frame of reference to a somewhat narrow economic approach as regards resources expansion and allocation. The problem of economic development, however, is admittedly a much braoder one. We have seen, even as we pursued the analytical issues involved in resources expansion and allocation, that we could not avoid relating our discussion to other facets of society's development as a whole. Even if I decide to stay away from many of the political, sociological and other aspects relevant to the aspiration for rapid economic development by the present-day underdeveloped countries, I may still be called upon to indicate, in a broader perspective, what I consider to be the basic economic conditions that have to be satisfied for the take-off, and to assess India's achievement in this regard.

Different countries are naturally beset with different problems or with similar problems in different degrees of urgency; but empirical observation of the countries concerned leads me to list the following five tasks as the most common desiderata for newly developing countries in the present historical juncture.

The liquidation of colonialism in the economic sphere. Of course, economic dependence as such is not decried here. What is at issue is the artificial suppression or one-sided development of economic potentialities of a country as a concomitant to the political subjugation. It has often been the case that the legacies of economic colonialism linger on after the attainment of political independence; and in such circumstances efforts to mobilize the maximum energy of the people for economic development tend to be thwarted.

Land reform. In majority cases, underdeveloped countries of today are characterized by the predominant position of agriculture in their economic structure and, furthermore, by the type of land tenure which subsumes a conflict of classes of one kind or another. Often the cultivating class is a doubly-exploited class; and for the release of suppressed energy of such a class for the nation-building in which they can feel the identification of interest, a radical measure of land reform is the order of the day.

"Big push" in the build-up of social overhead structures and other external economies. Having come into confrontation with this problem more than a century after the groping experience with it by the advanced countries, the present-day underdeveloped countries are in the position to appreciate the importance

73

of the "big push" and to plan the steps for it with a view to long range planning ahead. By nature, social overhead structures can more economically be laid out when planned with a longer time horizon, and thus the role of the state in this sphere is likely to be more important than elsewhere. It may be added that education, both general and technical, is to be conceived to fall under this category.

Laying out of rails for the lines of development of industries most suited for the country. Most underdeveloped countries specialize in one or the other primary industry which appears to be linked to the peculiar endowment in resources of the country. Abstractly a case could be made for the thesis that such a specialization be further encouraged. But the real world being what it is, what with the extreme instability of prices of primary products and what with specific income elasticities for different products, etc., the aspiration of young nations towards industrialization is perfectly rational, especially if we take a dynamic view on the fuller utilization of human elements in the resources endowment. The question then arises whether reliance on the market mechanism alone will enable a young nation to find its way to the choice of such new industries as most suited to itself. It is submitted here that the high threshold for successful establishment of a new manufacturing industry, due to the technological level required and to the volume of initial capital needed, makes it difficult to bring about a "break through" with the reliance on the market mechanism alone and that the deliberate "laying out of rails" is highly desirable.

Creation of the mechanism which extracts the surplus and channels it into productive investment. Any society beyond the stage of primitive technique is capable of producing the surplus over and above the customary subsistence level of that society. But depending on the institutional form the surplus takes, it may be dissipated or diverted to non-productive uses. What is needed is the development of social institutions in a community such that the maximum surplus consistent with other overriding considerations can be extracted and then channeled into productive investment. The mechanism in question can be, of course, of different types.

I believe that every one of these five tasks confronted India at the time of her gaining independence in 1947. To what extent she has been successful in tackling with these problems, I do not intend to discuss in this paper. But a general remark may be ventured here to say (a) that her mixed economy orientation apparently has induced her to go slowly especially on the second desideratum above and (b) that the strategy to tackle with these five tasks would have required concentrated efforts on a much more limited number of objectives than the well-rounded planning of India's Five-Year Plans decided to wrestle with. The problem of economic development today, in the era where the 19th century type of capitalistic development is no longer feasible, is, I believe, more a matter of pushing crudely chosen priorities than that of general equilibrium or operational research.

Chapter 5

THE ROLE OF THE CITY IN TECHNOLOGICAL INNOVATION AND ECONOMIC DEVELOPMENT

[1961]

Preliminary version of this essay was read on 25 July 1961 at the *Conference on the City and History* in Cambridge, Massachusetts. Subsequently, the Japanese version, somewhat modified, was published in the *Asahi Journal* (14 January 1962). This English version is here made public for the first time.

Introduction

The subject matter implied under the title calls for an especially balanced integration of empirical, historical and analytical inquiries; and although various aspects of the problem have been explored, particularly in the last several years, by a large number of social scientists with some degrees of intensity, the frame of reference in which the issues are being discussed, it may be said, is still in a largely fluid condition. What I propose to do in this paper is to pursue only one aspect of the problem somewhat analytically—an aspect which I consider to be the most important in the general discussion of the role of the city in technological innovation and economic development. Although what follows is fairly abstract, it is intended to apply mainly to the last two centuries or to the future, and, furthermore, problems peculiar to the "urban frontier" type of situation are to be largely ignored. Deliberate creation of a city like Brasilia[1] has no doubt an important role to play in the developmental process; but this type of drastic discontinuity presents a special set of dynamic problems and these will be outside my purview.

Economic Significance of Cities

Agglomeration of population beyond a certain degree of density per area,[2] that is to say, emergence of a city, comes about with a certain minimum rise of productivity based on the division of labor. The division of labor depends, as Adam Smith

[1] Cf., for example, the following characterization of the Brazilia's purpose: "The second purpose of the new capital is to encourage development of the under-populated interior, which has vast resources waiting to be tapped...... It is hoped that the construction of a big city deep in the interior, with the markets it will create and the new movements of population it will stimulate, will start a far-reaching process of opening up the undeveloped areas. More significant even than markets and population are communications: it is chiefly the lack of communications that has held up the development of the interior. But already roads and railways link Brasilia with the coastal cities and—as important to the future development of the country—the new modern highway that leads to Brasilia is being continued northwards for another thousand miles, penetrating for the first time into the tropical jungle of the Amazon basin." (J.M. Richards, 'Brazil's New Capital City' *The Listener*, November 13, 1958, p.772.)

[2] Of course, it is impossible, and also unnecessary, to draw a hard and fast line on demographic density in defining a city for all purposes. If some indication is required, we might refer to the arbitrary level chosen by the Indian Census of 1951, i.e. "not less than one thousand inhabitants to the square mile." But this criterion will obviously fail in a country like Japan where farming is done so intensively that one square mile (256 hectares) of cultivable land often supports 320 farm families, or possibly 1440 inhabitants.

pointed out two centureis ago, upon the size of the market; and the size of the market, in turn, depends on productivity. Here is an instance of "circular causation"[3] which characterizes a large part of socio-economic phenomena, in particular the economic aspect of urbanization. In a particular situation it may be the progress in the division of labor which gives impetus to the emergence of a city as a market place or it may be the pre-existing agglomeration of people (for whatever reason) which gives stimulus to a further progress in the division of labor. Whichever it may be, the relation becomes mutually reinforcing for very good economic reasons. The progress of productivity in transportation and communication, which initially may have been stimulated by the economic logic of a market place, in turn enables expansion of the size of the market and this makes possible a further proliferation of the division of labor and consequently a rise in productivity.

The evolution of cities during the past three hundred years or so, which manifests clearly this mutually reinforcing character of their economic functions, has in its background the evolution of a socio-economic system which we call capitalism. Capitalism is essentially an order of atomistic units where profit-and-loss accounting in terms of each unit independently of any other provides a signal for action and where an order on the social scale, or even on the international scale, is presumably maintained through the "Invisible Hand" of unfettered competition. If the growth of cities is said to have its economic rationale, it can best be described in terms of a conceptual framework which separates out as "external economies" those positive contributions to the rise in productivity which cannot be directly attributed to the action of individual accounting unit in the system,

[3] See G. Myrdal, *Rich Lands and Poor*, 1957.

i.e., private individual firms. In other words, we may say that *the economic significance of cities lies in the external economies they provide.*

External Economies and Diseconomies

We shall pose here to clarify the concept of external economies and its counterpart, that of external diseconomies.

As the term ("external economies") was originally used by Alfred Marshall,[4] it was intended to refer to those economies arising from an increase in the scale of production which are "dependent on the general development of the industry" and not on "the resources of the individual houses of business engaged in it." His concern was mainly over the question of analyzing "the economies arising from an increase in the scale of production," and furthermore was restricted to *intra*-industry economies. As the term came to be used more and more, its application has been widened to cover *inter*-industry economies also, that is to say, the economies external to one industry due to the growth of other industries. And once we did so, it became apparent that the economies involved were not necessarily the function of the enlarged scale only.[5] The factor of inter-industry complementarities has come to be recognized as equally, if not more, important. Thus we now use the term "external economies" to cover all those interstitial economies, either technical or pecuniary,[6] which arise independently of the resources of atomistic firms. If a subway line is opened,

---

[4] See A. Marshall, *Principles of Economics*, Eighth ed., p.266.

[5] It must be stated that Marshall himself was aware of this. See *ibid.*, p.441.

[6] If external economies enable a firm to reduce the real input per unit-output, they are "technical." If they enable a firm to reduce the cost of unit input, they are "pecuniary."

the surface intersection which opens to a subway station will suddenly become a busy intersection and the retailing opportunities will be enhanced. The location in this case has a complementarity value in connecting the transportation system with an office area or a residential section as the case may be; and we speak of the benefits enjoyed by retailers as "external economies."

As the example just offered enables us to see, external economies can be appropriated by a private economic unit. A corner drug-store at the intersection of a subway stop will suddenly be able to expand its sales; and, within limits, the store-keeper has a choice of lowering mark-up profits on goods he sells and thus expand the radius of his customer-area or garner a greater absolute volume of profit with prices unchanged. When he has such a choice, the site value of land also rises; and if there is to be a transfer in ownership of that piece of land, the appropriation of external economies takes place partly in the form of capital gains. This kind of thing is wholly predictable. Thus it is quite conceivable that a subway company intending to develop a line buy up strategic pieces of land in advance and then lay out the line, reaping capital gains on the land value. This is a type of situation which is called "the internalization of external economies."

Just as there arise cases of external economies through complementarities of all kinds, we cannot avoid having cases of external diseconomies through concurrence of incidents in a particular situation. Pigou's classical example refers to the nuisance suffered by housewives living near a factory with an active smoke-stack in their attempt to dry laundries outdoors. In this case, the households may be compensated for the inconvenience through a lower house rent. But external diseconomies which arise in a modern city, about which we shall discuss later in a more detail, are in fact so complex nowadays in their nexus of causation that the extent of compensatory accounting expected of private individual economic units is extremely limited. In other words, in a private enterprise economy, the problem of "internalization" has not been symmetric as regards external economies and diseconomies. The following observation by Hirschman, although it refers mainly to the nineteenth century capitalism, expresses this point eloquently:

> "From the point of view of investment incentives, the capitalist system, especially as it existed in the nineteenth century, is hard to beat: there was a minimum of internalization of external diseconomies and there was no limitation on the internalization of pecuniary external economies through acquisitions, combinations, or mergers with closely interdependent economic activities."[7]

From the social point of view, a certain combination of socio-economic incidents may involve both external economies and diseconomies and we may abstractly be able to speak of *net* economies or diseconomies of *external* character. The contention of this paper, in a bare outline, is that:

(1) In the early stage of capitalistic development, cities provided a large measure of external economies which could be privately appropriated, and thus they had a strong economic rationale;

(2) With the development of modern technology, some of the erstwhile external economies came to be diluted while external diseconomies became more and more substantial; and thus it is becoming increasingly uncertain if there are still net external economies or not.

[7] A.O. Hirschman, *The Strategy of Economic Development*, 1958, p.58.

(3) Society's concern on external diseconomies has become more and more heightened; and some degree of their internalization is now expected of private firms.

(4) The very indivisibilities, which contribute to the peculiar complementarities, thus to the external economies, observed in cities, make it difficult for established cities to adjust themselves without incurring heavy cost to the requirements of dynamic technological changes. Thus planning for urban renewal today constitutes a particularly challenging field which calls for an integrated efforts of several disciplines as well as a marriage of forward-looking vision with factual analysis.

External Economies of Cities

What are some of the external economies which we can commonly observe in the agglomeration of population in modern times? They, of course, differ in relative importance depending on different phases of capitalistic development, correlated as they are to changing technological innovations. But for general purposes we may enumerate the following aspects:

(1) The city as a nerve-center of commercial activities

(2) The city itself as a market

(3) The city as an industrial center

As the division of labor progresses with the extention of market, the act of commerce, which is implied in this situation, begins naturally to call for a nerve-center. And such a nerve-center will be economically the more efficient, the more of external economies it can draw from (a) the convenient network of transportation and port facilities and of communications, (b) financial institutions in aid of commerce, and (c) the proximity to the source of information which enables the act of commerce to have better expectations. The last item would include, among other things, the nearness to a political and administrative center; and in some countries, it is of considerable significance. For example in Japan, the external economies emanating from this source are of sufficient value that practically every commercial firm whose otherwise convenient seat of operation is in Osaka finds it necessary, as well as worthwhile, to incur cost in setting up a significant-size branch office in Tokyo, four hundred miles away, for information-gathering purposes.

That the city itself constitutes a convenient market for consumers' goods is obvious. Not only the density of population but also a certain demonstration effect common in urban life help create special external economies for sellers of a large number of items of mass consumption goods. It is as regards services, however, that the city as a market provides unique external economies. Services are by nature non-transportable. A barber can be transported; but barber's service has to be accepted at the site and at the moment of its performance. Agglomeration of population makes it possible for various services industries to grow with the fixed site of operation. And especially since the city tends, in the heyday of capitalism, to become the residential site for the élite class, whose demand for various forms of services is generally high, the city provides unique external economies for the tertiary industry as a whole. This relation *ipso facto* reinforces the agglomeration and has a reinforcing effect on the city as a market. It is a universally observed fact that the occupational composition of urban labor force is highly slanted towards the tertiary industry.

External economies provided by the city in giving locational

83

convenience for industrial establishments were of unique importance especially in the early stage of capitalistic development. An industrial factory requires the supply, in a fairly dense concentration, of wage laborers who are "free" not only in the sense of "free to enter into the wage contract with an employer" but also in the sense of "free from attachment to the means of production such as land property." The agglomeration of population, which constitutes a city, provides such a supply, either as an antecedent condition for, or as a consequence of, the establishment of factories. Then, there is also a need, by modern industrial establishments, for easy access to the supply of qualified personnel, such as engineers and other staff members; and it is doubtless easier to recruit these people in the city because of its cultural, educational and medical facilities which such people especially care about. Both of these external economies mentioned here, however, may not be so important now as in the early days of capitalist development. Technological developments, in the sphere of transportation and communications, as well as the aggravating multiplication of external diseconomies in a large city, have contributed to an increasing trend of dispersion of industrial establishments. Nevertheless, it still remains to be true that so far as the external economy of transportation and communication facilities is concerned, it continues to be a controlling factor for industrial establishments today as it was crucial for them in the early stage.

The external economies of cities, mentioned here, become the object of "internalization" and thus enhance the profitability of private business situated in cities, and/or they yield a room for what Schumpeter used to call "interference of income"[8] and help support varied categories of tertiary employment. In either case, economic rationale of cities is thus strengthened. This picture of cities prospering on external economies, however, is relevant largely to capitalist societies of a generation or more ago. Various technological developments, starting with the effective use of electric power and the mass use of automobiles, have given rise to a new configuration of forces, working very often in a centrifugal manner in relation to erstwhile centers of population agglomeration. The current flowering of innovations, which are for good reason characterized as "scientific-industrial revolution," no doubt has far-reaching implications on the nature of external economies of cities discussed above. It is not intended to speculate on them here; but at least it appears to be certain that classical types of external economies of cities will be further modified and that the city planning of this new era will call for special insight into implications for it of latest technological changes.

Social Cost Accounting of External Economies and Diseconomies of Cities

It is the essence of the private enterprise economy that the cost accounting is self-contained with respect to each economic unit. Otherwise, imputation of profit to atomistic units is not possible. External economies and diseconomies of cities do imply both benefits, which may or may not be internalized,

---

[8] Where there is an opportunity to internalize external economies to yield large profit, such profit tends to be shared by intermediaries who "interfere" by claiming income to themselves on the basis of their specialized service. A pecuniarily important part of the function of real estate dealers partakes of the character of this phenomenon.

and costs, which again may or may not be internalized. Furthermore, municipalities, too, are not in the habit of making a balance sheet on them.

Take, for example, cost implications of external economies. It has been suggested by some that a part of the historical explanation for the North-South economic disparity in Italy is the somewhat one-sided expenditure by the central government in the North for defense purposes. All the garrisons were in the North. Military roads were constructed in the North. And even the arsenal which used to be located in Naples was moved to the North for the reason that Naples was vulnerable to bombing from the sea. All these things helped generate external economies for industrial development in the North; but the cost for them was, by nature, shared by the nation as a whole. In fact, the regressive character of the Italian tax system at the time caused the South, it is most likely, to pay for it more than the pro rata share in terms of its value-added production. Here, then, is a case of one region enjoying certain external economies the cost for which was paid by another region.

This, of course, is nothing unusual when one is dealing with the problem of external economies. A large part of social overhead structures, which created external economies, is built or established by governmental bodies through the use of public funds. And in most cases, even the *direct* beneficiaries of them are not expected to pay in strict accordance with the benefit they receive, let alone the *indirect* beneficiaries who enjoy external economies incidental to the existence of such structures.

As regards external diseconomies, however, it is noteworthy that there has been a fairly well-marked evolution in capitalist societies in their attitudes on the need to counteract them as well as on the question of who is to bear the burden of cost for counteracting them. There was a time, as reported by Walter Quebedeaux, Jr.,[9] when a smoke-abatement law was strictly enforced in England, so much so that one violator of the law, which prohibited the use of coal as detrimental to health, was prosecuted, condemned and executed. But this was in 1307, that is, some time before a modern capitalist society came into being. As capitalism evolved, it nurtured the philosophy of *laissez-faire*, according to which atomistic economic units were to be left free to pursue the aim of maximizing their own respective profit untrammelled by controls or interferences of the government. "The Invisible Hand" was to take care of the task of harmonizing conflicting interests for social welfare. It is this stage of capitalism to which the characterization by Hirschman, quoted earlier, is relevant, to wit: "there was a minimum of internalization of external diseconomies."

There are, however, two forces which have changed the picture substantially in the recent decades. One is the series of technological developments which have contributed towards aggravating external diseconomies of cities, and the other is the increasing public concern over such diseconomies and the emerging climate of public opinion in favor of private firms' internalizing some of these external diseconomies. These two forces, combined together, have given rise to the secondary, but no less important, consequence of exodus from cities of upper income families and some of private concerns, thereby "increasing the complexities cities must cope with and decreasing the resources with which they must do the coping."[10]

[9] In a paper read before a session of the 54th Annual Meeting of the Air Pollution Control Association on June 12, 1961.

[10] Joseph S. Clark, "To Come to the Aid of Their Cities" *New York Times Magazine*, April 30, 1961, p.11.

What are some of the external diseconomies which have become more and more serious lately? Air pollution, of course, is at least as old as the first smoke-abatement law of England of 1273. But the degree of pollution today is incomparably more serious, especially with a countless number of automobiles emitting fumes into the city air.[11] Water pollution, on the other hand, may be said to be less of a problem for most cities inasmuch as cities nowadays are equipped with hygienic water systems for which necessary expenditures are not spared. We find, however, here and there cases of rapidly growing cities which suffer from chronic water shortage with which they seem never to be able to catch up. Tapping of subterranean water in such circumstances has created a serious problem of ground-level subsidence in some cities. Next, the traffic problem looms probably as a most serious diseconomy of modern cities with high density of automobile use. Diseconomy here could be counteracted by the expenditure of sufficient amount of money for multi-level intersection roads, tunnels, underground parking lots, etc. To the extent this is the case, the diseconomy is translated into additional cost for users. But even then, the speed with which one can exit from the center of a city cannot but be affected by congestion;[12] and it is not easy to retain the beauty of city landscape when a structural monster of multi-level intersection intrudes in the interest of the traffic convenience. Less direct than the above in their logical connection with the agglomeration of population are such manifestations of external diseconomies as slum areas and

[11] It may be noted in this connection that New York City finally warned major autombile manufacturers on June 4, 1961, to install anti-fume device on their new cars voluntarily or run the risk of being compelled to do so. Previous to this, the Automobile Manufacturers Association had rejected a request by the Secretary of Health, Education and Welfare that the industry install the anti-pollution device.

[12] Cf. *Fortune*, October 1957, pp.158–9.

juvenile delinquency; but these are nonetheless characteristic of modern cities along with varied forms of vice, notably the organized gambling which in many cities of the world defies the law or, still worse, is in collusion with the agent of the law.

Even in a society where the private enterprise system is dominant, it cannot be denied, general awareness of external diseconomies has lately been heightened and the public opinion is becoming more and more crystallized in the direction of favoring either the direct internalization of external diseconomies by private enterprises or the sharing by residents of cost incurred by municipalities in counteracting such diseconomies. But even so, the financial capability of geographically defined municipal governments is becoming increasingly inadequate in coping with the problem; and advocates of federal assistance in this regard are rapidly increasing in number.[13] What is required now seems to be a new frame of reference in dealing with economic problems of cities such that their social cost accounting can be rationally spelled out in the light of latest technological development which affect the configuration of a modern metropolis. When this is done, it may turn out that the old idea of local autonomy, as well as the capitalistic tenet of self-contained atomistic accounting, is found to be somewhat obsolete.

Tasks for the Future

A speedway bypassing the downtown congestion would establish its usefulness only when it is completed over a sufficient distance. A railroad terminal in a city without the ancillary structures, such as side-tracks for freight and so on, would be

[13] Senator Joseph Clark's article, cited earlier, is an example of this trend.

like a school-building without class-rooms. In other words, many of the structures which contribute to the complementarities, which are observed in cities, do so because of their indivisibilities or, in a more expressive terminology, of their lumpiness. Furthermore, such structures are generally of durable type, lasting several decades or more for economic use. When a structure which contributes to external economies of a city is by nature lumpy and is at the same time durable for good reason, the marginal type of adjustment to a new situation, which is characteristic of a large part of rational economic action, has to be ruled out. Once a structure is built and completed, we will have to put up with it for some time even when we find that it stands in the way of adopting something new and better. Since municipalities are not run on the basis of private profit-and-loss accounting, one could say that the principle of accelerated obsolescence has a broad room for application here so long as they are capable of commanding sufficient financial resources. But here again, social cost accounting is in order; and the opportunity cost in social terms may be found to be quite exorbitant.

In fact, the point just enunciated is the reason why so many cities in the world suffer from the backlog of tasks for urban renewal in spite of the obvious obsolescence of structures and configurations in the face of technological and other developments which are diluting the erstwhile external economies and aggravating, or newly creating, external diseconomies. There is an additional reason, inherent in the system of private enterprise economy, for the difficulty of drastic, large-scale, adjustment. It stems from the fact that the existing complementarities create private vested interests in the form of opportunities for internalizing external economies—vested interests which are inextricably tied to the system of private ownership of land and structures. A large-scale urban renewal can easily shift the configuration of external economies and cause windfall profits to some and calamitous losses to others. Whenever a single act is capable of causing both and the compensation of loss by profits cannot easily be arranged, a stalemate is likely to be the result.

What, then, should we conclude from these observations in mapping our tasks for the future as cities become more and more enmeshed in the multiplying complexities of technological innovations?

Firstly, it appears to be obvious, but stands repeating, that the problem of cities today awaits co-operation of experts of several disciplines on a level far higher and more integrated than hitherto has been the case. It is my belief that in particular the role of economists in this co-operative task is to be much greater than they themselves have realized in the past.

Secondly, because of indivisibilities and durability of structures which form the basis of external economies of cities and because recurring technological innovations requires a new configuration of structures in order for net external economies to be maximized, a special degree of foresight and boldness, coupled with flexibility, is needed in the present-day city planning, and once a plan is decided on, its execution had better be steadfast and unflinching. A technologically most advanced city in a technologically most advanced country may not be able to avoid groping and fumbling; but others which follow should be able to learn from the lessons of the forerunner.

Thirdly, it might be proposed that economists interested in the problems of cities engage themselves in the empirical research on social cost accounting of external economies and diseconomies of modern cities. A comparative study of cities in capitalist societies and those in socialist ones is likely to be especially rewarding inasmuch as differing effects upon this problem of different modes of ownership of land and structural properties could thus be brought out.

Fourthly, as we focus more and more on the aspect of the problem which we call external economies and diseconomies, it is quite possible that we shall be led to call into question the rationality of atomistic cost accounting in the context of the present-day technological development. In fact, the very concept of *external* economies and diseconomies presupposes the dominant light in which we regard the atomistic cost accounting. Rethinking on the matter may well call for a new conceptual frame of reference in dealing with the cost-benefit implications of urban configuration. At the same time, self-contained accounting by a municipal unit with old boundaries may no longer be able to claim rationality in itself. Instead of visualizing a federal assistance, for example, as an "encroachment" on local autonomy or at best as something abnormal or extraordinary, we would do better, I think, if we turned over a new leaf on this question and reset our thinking in terms of the national responsibilities for metropolitan affairs in general. How to harmonize the tenet of decentralized decision-making with the increasing need of social and national orientation is a problem which taxes democratic societies today not solely in the sphere of urban problems.

Chapter 6

STRACHEY ON CAPITALISM

[1957]

This is a review article on John Strachey's *Contemporary Capitalism*, 1956, originally published in *Monthly Review*, 1957. The subject matter may sound somewhat heterogeneous in this collection; but its inclusion here reflects the author's belief that the qualitative aspect is, if at all, more important than the quantitative in the process of economic development.

Litvinoff's Prophesy

Franklin D. Roosevelt relates in a letter[1] he wrote to Thomas Lamont in 1942 an episode of his encounter with Maxim Litvinoff in the fall of 1933 when they were holding a series of discussions preliminary to the U.S. recognition of the Soviet Union. When F.D.R. found that Litvinoff was adamant against permitting professional clergymen to enter Russia even after renewing of diplomatic relations, he exploded in despair,

---

[1] *The Roosevelt Letters*, ed. by Elliott Roosevelt, George G. Harrap & Co., Vol. III, 1952, pp.444–45.

saying that "it is useless; we are poles apart!"   To this, Litvinoff
is quoted to have replied:

> I hope you will not feel that way, Mr. President, because I do not.
> In 1920 we were as far apart as you say.   At that time you were
> one hundred percent capitalistic and we were at the other extreme
> —zero.   In these thirteen years we have risen in the scale to, let
> us say, a position of twenty.   You Americans, especially since last
> March, have gone to a position of eighty.   It is my real belief that
> in the next twenty years we will go to forty and you will come down
> to sixty.   I do not believe the rapprochement will get closer than
> that.   And while it is difficult for nations to confer with and
> understand each other with a difference between twenty and
> eighty, it is wholly possible for them to do so if the difference is
> only between forty and sixty.

F.D.R. adds a comment that "Litvinoff's answer is worthy of
an eventual place in history."

More than twenty years have passed since the time of this
episode; and in a significant sense we are tempted to agree with
the F.D.R.'s comment.   Although the reality of the cold war
has given the appearance of severer conflict than ever between
the leader countries of the two camps, capitalism and socialism
as *economic systems* seem to have come much closer to each other
than a generation ago.   Especially in the post-war period,
capitalism has learned to adapt itself through a greater degree
of control by government over key economic quantities; and
socialism, on the other, has shown a distinct sign of evolution by
making increasing use of the price mechanism and the principle
of local initiative.   Even the matter of public ownership of the
means of production, which was once regarded as crucial in
distinguishing the two systems, seems to have lost its pristine
significance.   Take, for example, countries like Austria and
India where the nationalized sector is relatively quite large; we

do not speak of them yet as socialist economies. Few people would doubt the truth of Litvinoff's remark that the two systems, even after closing their gap as nearly as 60 to 40, should and can be distinguished from each other in essential respects. But at the same time a question is asked more and more as to what really distinguishes socialism from capitalism so far as *economic* aspects are concerned.

Strachey's Arguments

Strachey's book,[2] which we understand constitutes only the first volume of a bigger enterprise, is a timely contribution which attempts essentially to answer the problem just raised. He starts his analysis by characterizing the latest stage of capitalism as "an economy of large and few units" (oligopoly). This circumstance necessarily brings about "the metamorphosis of competition" with a result that these oilgopolists acquire a power to affect prices of their products, thus enabling them to affect the level of their own profits also. The degree of ecomonic concentration thus attained renders the self-regulating market mechanism unworkable and opens the gate to a much greater degree of state intervention in the affairs of economy than used to be tolerated in the past. This state intervention, however, could be *either* in the nature of social control on behalf of the population as a whole *or* designed to benefit mainly the class of oligopolistic capitalists. Which way it turns depends on the consolidation of the democratic forces in the country concerned. Democracy, whose essence is the diffusion of power throughout the community, has proved itself capable of counteracting even the so-called law of increas-

[2] John Strachey, *Contemporary Capitalism*, 1956.

ing misery of the working class; and *"if it can maintain itself,* [it] will in fact transform latest-stage capitalism in the end out of existence."* (p. 313) For democracy to be effective, however, a society has to be economically over the "hump" in the sense that it has already surmounted the initial stage of industrialization and has attained a level of annual per-capita income above $250 or so.

Strachey's theme is clearly one of *political economy;* in fact, admirably so. On the one hand, he appears to be well aware of the importance of analyzing the objective laws and tendencies of an economic system called capitalism—the laws and tendencies which can be in the first instance stated independently of ideas and aspirations of individual members of the system. Upon these he makes impinge the conscious political force of democratic pressure (which is visualized in turn as closely related to a certain level of economic attainment) and relies on its success even in the crucial task of transforming capitalism into socialism. It may be said, therefore, that the main task for a critic here is to examine if Strachey's reliance on democratic pressure is not simply a wishful thinking, that is to say, if it can be demonstrated as objectively well-grounded. His conception of the state as a neutral receptacle of political power is, of course, not new; and the issue has been debated repeatedly in the past.[3] A new context in which he couches the issue certainly calls for its re-examination. But more basic in this connection, it appears to me, is his understanding of the essential economic characteristic of capitalism as distinguished from that of socialism, for it could easily be that the failure to pursue this latter distinction to the fullest lead one to exaggerate the malleability

---

[3] See P.M. Sweezy, *The Theory of Capitalist Development*, 1942, 349–52.

of the capitalistic state machine. It is proposed, therefore, that in what remains of this article we concentrate our discussion on the basic economic issue.

What Distinguishes One Economic System from Another

Let us pose our question in the following manner: what is it that distinguishes different economic systems from each other? I believe that the most fruitful approach is to ask another question and to try to answer it, namely: *who controls the surplus?* Any society which has progressed in overall productivity beyond the stage of satisfying the bare necessity for its members can be said to have the potentiality of producing the surplus. With a further progress in productive powers, what is generally regarded as the bare necessity may gradually change both in quantity and quality and so is the size of a potential surplus. Such is the *technical* aspect of the surplus which could be discussed more or less independently of the type of economic system at issue. There is, however, another aspect to the surplus, the institutional aspect, which is inextricably related to the specific form of economic organization. For example, under the feudal system the surplus is appropriated by the feudal ruling class and is disposed of in the characteristic manner; under capitalism it takes the form of "surplus value" appropriated by the capitalist class and is again disposed of in the manner characteristic to the system. Such characteristics of the surplus which are uniquely related to a particular system in question are generally referred to as the *form* of the surplus, and it can easily be shown that the *manner of disposal* of the surplus is closely related to the form, and even the *size* of the surplus, which appears to be deter-

97

mined mainly by technological conditions, is often a function of the form.

Let us draw out further implications of this approach by applying it to the comparison of socialism with capitalism. Under socialism the surplus partakes the form of a social fund, and within limits given by technological conditions its size is an object of social control, being directly determined by the size of investment which is centrally planned. If the central planning authorities decide, for some reason, to lower the level of investment, they can do so by appropriately lowering prices of consumer goods thus automatically reducing the size of the surplus to the required level. The reduction of the surplus constitutes no hindrance to the attainment of full utilization of resources. Under capitalism, however, the surplus takes the form essentially of profit; and each unit of investment depends upon a micro-decision which is profit-motivated. Thus the profit realized constitutes justification for an investment decision taken. Although *aggregatively* it may be said, as Keynesian economists do nowadays, that the volume of investment determines the size of profit even under capitalism, it should be noted that it does so via causing a fluctuation in the level of economic activities at the same time. In the circumstance where the surplus takes the form of profit which acts as the prime motive force of engines of the system, the crucial question is *whether the condition of full employment can be sustained without high profit*. If the answer is negative, as I believe it is, it will be difficult for capitalism to adjust itself to the requirements of a historical stage in its development where a high propensity to consume is called for. For a high profit economy is a high investment economy and a high investment economy is an economy of rapid and constant change. In Schumpeter's words: "whereas a stationary feudal economy would still be a feudal economy, and a stationary socialist economy would still be a socialist economy, stationary capitalism is a contradiction in terms."[4]

Strachey Criticized

I have taken some space to develop my ideas on the criterion for differentiating economic systems in order to make it easier to bring Strachey's position into relief. Let me first quote one of the relevant passages from his book. He writes:

> It is becoming clear that what chiefly determines the standard of life of the mass of the population is not the social *form* taken by accumulation, e.g., whether it be private profit or a social fund, but its *amount*. In other words, at any given level of national productivity, what in the main determines the national standard of life is not whether accumulation takes the form of private property or a social fund, but whether the rate of accumulation is set high or low. (p. 238, Italics in the original)

This passage seems to indicate that Strachey takes such an optimistic view of what "democratic pressure" can do that so long as the *amount* of the surplus can be raised high and sustained high, the *form* is of little significance and the rest can be taken care of by "the democratic action of the people." He even goes on to say that "what the democratic mechanism is forcing governments, more or less unconsciously, to attempt is, in a word, the socialization of investment." (p. 259)

The position indicated here would be more acceptable if Strachey had taken a fuller account of the type of analysis I sketched in the preceding section and had specified the manner

---

[4] J.A. Schumpeter, "Capitalism in the Postwar World," *Postwar Economic Problems*, ed. by S.E. Harris, 1943, pp.116–17.

in which "the democratic mechanism" could cope with the objective economic constraints implied in the particular *form* of the surplus. I believe that he failed to do this. Take, for example, the point that since under capitalism savers and investors are different agents, *ex ante* saving and actual investment may diverge, and the divergence tends to have a cumulative effect and to cause fluctuations in output and employment. This set of relations is what I would call "an objective economic constraint" flowing out of the fact that the surplus under capitalism takes the particular *form* of private profit. Strachey admits the existence of this set of relations but calls it "a monstrous contingency" and observes that "it is this monstrous contingency, even more than private profit, that 'puts off' the present electorate from accepting a high rate of accumulation." (p. 245) The passage like this makes one doubt if Strachey pursued sufficiently the implications of what he himself called "the social form taken by accumulation." We may point out further that under capitalism, where the prime motive force of engines of the system is private profit, there is always, and in an increasing measure, *a pressure to sell* which causes the emergence of a whole host of unproductive labor. This circumstance is especially conspicuous in the United States and makes it impossible for us to accept, without further analysis, a proposition like the one implied in the earlier quotation from Strachey to the effect that the national standard of life is higher the higher the rate of accumulation is. As a matter of fact, I am inclined to believe that the continued prosperity of a country like the United States has depended, in a large measure, upon the institutionalization of various kinds of *waste* (such as defense expenditures, selling cost, the acceleration of obsolescence, etc.) and that this trend is inherent in the capitalist mode of production.

In short, both on theoretical and empirical grounds, I feel that the form of the surplus pertaining to a particular system of economy is not so malleable as Strachey makes out to be, and accordingly that the task of a political economist would require a much greater degree of realism than it is manifested in the Strachey's book on the possibilities and limitations of the democratic mechanism within the framework of capitalistic constraints.

A Suggestion

Vision of what is to come in human society, however, often emanates from a person who is prone to minimize what appears to be the objective limitations. In this sense, there are much that can be learned from occasional remarks in the Strachey's book. Take, for example, the following passage:

> What has to be done is to provide some way in which the system's mainspring, namely, investment in new means of production, can be undertaken at a rational rate, without interruption, and independently of fluctuation in the expectation of profit-making. If—but only if—that can be done, much of the rest of the economic mechanism can, if this is convenient or expedient, be left in private hands to be operated under the hope of profit and the fear of loss. (p. 249)

In the light of what we have said earlier, this paragraph may be cited as another example of Strachey's inclination to slight the *form* of the surplus. But if we concentrate only on the first half of the paragraph (adding, however, a clause: "in directions consistent with the long range welfare of the people as a whole"), we may say that here we are given a vision of a strategy for evolutionary socialism which should be explored much more seriously than before, namely, to subject the *flow* of surplus under social control rather than to change the ownership of the surplus-generating *stock of capital* into public hands. Such a strategy would involve a greater use of price control techniques on intermediate goods and of recouping of surplus in the form of indirect taxes on consumer goods. It would be a strategy that could be applied by degrees, gradually changing its character from the socialization of the flow into that of the stock. If Strachey had been thinking something of this type of policy measures, I hope that he will develop and discuss more practical aspects of these measures in future instalments of his enterprise. Socialists residing in other capitalist countries will benefit greatly from such explorations on his part.

II. JAPAN'S EXPERIENCE

Chapter 7

THE TAKE-OFF OF JAPAN, 1868–1900

[1960]

Preliminary version of this essay was read by proxy at the Konstanz meeting of the International Economic Association in September 1960 and was subsequently published in *The Economics of Take-off into Sustained Growth*, 1963, edited by W.W. Rostow. The author benefited greatly from the discussion which took place on the paper at the meeting and which appeared in a summary form in the above volume.

The Essential Meaning of Take-off Interpreted

1. Since I am not quite yet ready to share with Rostow his stages-of-growth theory in its entirety, it is proposed to discuss at the outset my own interpretation of what Rostow essentially appears to mean by the expression of "take-off".

One technical condition for take-off, that the rate of productive investment has to rise from somewhere around 5 per cent to over 10 per cent of national income, is obvious enough. But this investment-income ratio is not uniquely related to a particular level of men's productivity in begetting material goods. The same level of productivity-mix could be associated with a low investment economy or a high investment economy. In the former case, it might be that wasteful consumption in the form of arms or conspicuous consumption by the privileged class is high; and in the latter case, it could be that the institutional constraint provides a mechanism of keeping average consumption level down to a bare minimum. For any given society one could think of a certain minimum level of current basic consumption, customarily conditioned by the taste and mores of that society at that time, over and above which, to the extent available, can be designated as surplus. Surplus can be utilized in a number of alternative ways, such as (a) for wars, (b) for conspicuous consumption by the privileged class, (c) as earnings to be repatriated to a mother country, (d) for shifting the general consumption level upwards, (e) for productive investment, and (f) may even be given away. The essential condition for take-off seems to be that there be created a mechanism in the society such that surplus will be habitually channelled into productive investment instead of being consumed in some other way.[1]

2. As a matter of approximation it can be stated, I believe, that the surplus takes different *forms* in different types of society. Under the feudal system, it is appropriated by the feudal ruling

[1] Rostow's thesis that there has to be a productivity rise in agriculture in the transitional process between a traditional society and a successful take-off and that "the rate of increase in output in agriculture may set the limit within which the transition to modernization proceeds" (*The Stages of Economic Growth*, p. 23) does not seem to me to be essential. Japan's case may provide us with a test. It is doubtful if physical productivity per land-area for any particular crop-product rose in any significant measure before the decade of the 1890's. Total physical output per agricultural family did rise through a better use of the slack-season hours, as well as through a more intensive utilization of dependents' labour, in producing a more diversified list of products. But it is significant that average real income of peasants showed practically no rise, again, until the decade of 1890s.

class and is disposed of in a characteristic manner. Under capitalism it takes the form essentially of profit. And under socialism, it may be said, the surplus takes the form of a social fund whose size, within limits given by technological conditions, is an object of social control. The fact that the size, as well as the manner of disposal, of the surplus is intimately related to a particular form the surplus takes is a matter of great importance. In a capitalist society privately-owned capital constitutes a basic unit of economic activities; and its essential quality is to expand itself continually. Capital which remains stagnant or which does not beget itself in an ever expanding manner does not justify itself as capital.[2] Thus under capitalism, profit, which in a broad sense of the term is the form of the surplus there, constitutes the major motivating force for advancing economic activities; and when it is realized, it is essentially under the control of private capital, and is generally destined for investment. Therefore, once capitalism is established, and so long as it is vigorous and viable, it may be said that growth is a built-in characteristic of the system.

3. We repeat, then, that the essential condition for take-off is that there be created a mechanism in the society such that surplus will be habitually channelled into productive investment instead of being consumed away. In the case of the People's Republic of China this is being achieved by means of the control of the surplus with an explicitly-stated precept that "the rise of

[2] When Schumpeter remarked: 'Unlike other economic systems, the capitalist system is geared to incessant economic change......Whereas a stationary feudal economy would still be a feudal economy, and a stationary socialist economy would still be a socialist economy, stationary capitalism is a contradiction in term's ("Capitalism in the Postwar World" in *Postwar Economic Problems*, edited by S.E. Harris, pp.116–7), he undoubtedly must have had in mind this self-expanding character of private capital.

productivity shall be faster than the rise of real wage". In the case of the Federation of Malaya it could be achieved by somehow making it obligatory for the entrenched foreign capital to reinvest their profit in Malaya instead of repatriating it abroad.[3] The take-off of Japan, of course, has already taken place; and the dominant fact of the situation, I believe, was that Japan developed into a capitalist economy sometime during the latter half of the nineteenth century and that with the progress of capitalism what Rostow calls "the compound interest" came to be sustained. In other words, to discuss the take-off of Japan is first to ask such questions as: (a) how was the milieu favourable to the capitalistic development prepared; for example, the spreading of money economy, the construction of social overhead capital, etc.? (b) how was the mechanism developed to mobilize financial resources to be channelled into productive investment in the hands of industrial capitalists? And whence did such resources come? (c) how did the supply of capitalistic entrepreneurs emerge? (d) how did the supply of workers emerge—the type of workers who were amenable to the discipline of modern industrial factories? and (e) how were the technological innovations needed for sustained growth brought about? It may be seen that some of these questions are equivalent to the problems highlighted by Rostow in connection with the "pre-condition" stage as well as with the "take-off" stage. But his theoretical framework is different from mine, and it will be dangerous to stress any particular equivalence too much. Thus what I propose to do with what follows is to pre-

[3] During the five years, 1949–53, the average annual repatriation of profits and interest away from Malaya amounted to $18.8 per capita of Malayan population. (See *The Economic Development of Malaya*, Report of a Mission Organized by the International Bank for Reconstruction and Development, 1955). Compare this figure with the average per capita investment figure of $5 to $10 in most of the south-east Asiatic countries.

sent my views on the characteristic aspect of Japan's take-off period in an attempt to indicate, in terms mainly of my own framework, the essential factors which seem to me to have contributed to Japan's attaining of growth-sustained economy. Occasions will be taken to comment on Rostow's thesis as I go along.

Characteristics of Japanese Capitalism in its Initial Stage: Ancillary Factors Considered

4. Since this essay is not meant to be a full treatment of the subject of capitalistic development in Japan, it may be advisable to give here a brief account of some of the relevant factors in the situation.

First, the matter of chronological orientation. Ports were opened for external trade in 1859. But the real political turning point was the Restoration of 1868 which brought to the top an entirely new leadership committed strongly to what Rostow calls "reactive nationalism". The period from 1868 to 1881 was that of post-Restoration reforms and continuing internal strifes (a major civil war broke out in 1877) culminating in the inflation of 1877–81. The Matsukata deflation of 1881–85, often suggested to be comparable to the English Restriction Period of 1815–21,[4] prepared the ground in many ways for the orderly functioning of capitalistic enterprises. A decade subsequent to this deflation period, i.e. 1886–1895, was the

[4] Schumpeter wrote on the English Restriction Period as follows: "As it was, policy consisted in providing a secure frame for entrepreneurial activity, in reducing burdens and fetters to a minimum and in defending this system with energy—ruthless energy, even—against outbreaks of discontent and misery." *Business Cycles*, 1939, p. 266. This description applies perfectly to the Matsukata deflation.

period of extremely rapid growth in the economy, especially in mechanised cotton spinning, the terminal year being the year Japan ended her war against China with victory. Rostow considers Japan's take-off period to cover roughly the twenty years between 1880 and 1900.

Next, a few points of relevance may be mentioned in the sphere of international economic relations. Until Japan's victory in the Sino-Japanese War which brought her the windfall of a large indemnity payment in gold and sterling,[5] there was only an insignificant inflow of foreign capital permitted during the first thirty years of new Japan. On the other hand, outflow of specie was sizeable until 1881, needed for the balancing of her current trade accounts. It should also be noted that Japan was *de facto* on the silver standard until 1897 and undoubtedly her exports benefited from the depreciation of silver against gold in 1890's.[6] That Japan did not gain her tariff autonomy until 1899, freeing herself from the 5 per cent limitation imposed upon her under a pre-Restoration agreement with foreign powers, is also a feature of her take-off period to be remembered.

5. A brief statistical summary is also in order. The best available study on Japan's growth rate[7] shows that the average annual growth-rate of real national income, based on the com-

[5] It amounted to ¥364,000,000, equivalent to about one-third of Japan's national income at the time.

[6] G. Droppers, commenting on the government's move for adopting the gold standard, wrote in 1896: If she [Japan] succumbs to the mania for gold at the present moment when her entire economic progress is a demonstration of the blessings of silver, she will have forgotten the lessons of experience precisely at the moment when they are most apparent and of the greatest utility to her." (*The Far East*, Vol. 1, No. 2, March 20, 1896, p. 21)

[7] K. Ohkawa and others, *The Growth Rate of the Japanese Economy since 1878*, 1957, p. 21.

parison of overlapping decades, was 4.3 per cent for 1878–87 to 1883–92, 4.9 per cent for 1883–92 to 1888–97, and 5.5 per cent for 1888–97 to 1893–1902. If these estimates are even roughly correct, they imply, on the assumption of a capital-output ratio of, say, 3, the net investment to income ratio of 13 to 16 per cent in the last quarter of the nineteenth century. As for the trend of price movements, a substantial degree of inflation is indicated during the three decades preceding the Restoration of 1868,[8] then an unsettled condition is observed during the first ten years of the new regime followed by the inflation of 1877–81. The succeeding Matsukata deflation brought down the general price level nearly to the pre-inflation level; and after 1886 the index[9] moved in the following manner:

1886	100	1892	124
1887	103	1893	115
1888	104	1894	122
1889	113	1895	131
1890	130	1896	141
1891	121	1897	156

The index kept on rising steadily to 388 in 1929 and 628 in 1941. In comparison with other capitalist countries, a generally inflationary trend is marked throughout the period of industrial development in Japan.

6. One other preliminary point has to cocupy us before we proceed to our central task of attempting to explain Japan's

[8] The price index for rice, with the average of 1830–46 as 100, stood at 404 in 1868 and the similar index for ginned cotton was 279 in 1868. (See T. Nawa, *Nihon Bosekigyo to Genmen Mondai Kenkyu*, 1937, pp. 156–7.)

[9] The index compiled by Ohkawa and others, but its base shifted from 1928–32 to 1886. See Ohkawa and others, *op. cit.*, p. 130.

take-off; and that is, the preoccupation of Restoration leaders with all the things implied in the "reactive nationalism" and the progress made in rounding out social overhead capital.

The preoccupation referred to dictated the policy of shunning the importation of foreign capital and expressed itself in the eagerness to introduce, and to assimilate, the advanced arts of western countries; but above all, it reflected itself in the peculiarly armament-oriented policy of industrial development. In a sense, this was a legacy of the pre-Restoration *bakufu* (central feudal) and clan governments which, partly for their internal political reasons, vied with each other in introducing modern weapons and the means to make them. It is significant that before a single cotton spinning machine was imported or a single mile of railroad was built the construction of a reverberatory furnace was completed (1852), a lathe-machine was imported (1856), and a shipyard was constructed to make steam-run warships (1863). The new regime intensified its efforts in this direction further by enunciating, in 1880, the policy of self-sufficiency in the production of armaments in both semi-finished and finished stages. From that time onwards, a characteristic situation prevailed in Japan that arms requirements played the role of an axis which, with generous government subsidies, tended to pull key heavy industries up to the standard dictated by military purposes.[10]

[10] In 1880 was invented the "Murata" rifle, the first rifle made in Japan, which was later (1885) perfected into a magazine rifle. In 1881, Osaka Iron Works was established by a Hunter, an employee in the Japanese Navy; and Naval Ordnance Factory in Tsukiji, Tokyo, adopted the Krupp method, commencing the production of steel. In 1882, Osaka Arsenal started producing bronze-steel in order to make Japan self-sufficient in copper. Also in 1882, the Kamaishi Iron Works was opened by the government. In 1883, the Kyodo Transport Company was established under government sponsorship, one of the main purposes being the strengthening of naval defence. The first vessel above 1,000 tons, Kosuga maru, was built at the Nagasaki Dockyard in this year,

Rounding out social overhead capital in its broadest sense also bears the mark of the nationalistic concern of government leaders. Railroad building was not to be entrusted to the hands of foreigners or private individuals. Although the first stretch of railroad, 18 miles long, was built (1872) with the aid of British capital and of foreign engineers, the first line constructed entirely by Japanese (the Keishin Line, 11 miles long, between Kyoto and Otsu) was completed (1880) before Japan had a total mileage of railroad of less than 100. The mileage grew after this at the rate of doubling every three years or faster, to attain the total of 1,880 miles by 1892. The landmarks in the development of modern means of communication were the commencing of governmental postal service in 1871, the introduction of telegraph in 1869 and the setting up of a public corporation for the service in1872, and the installation of the first telephone line in 1877. Unique in the administrative set-up of the Restoration government was the Kobu Sho (Department of Industrial Matters), which, though short-lived (1870–85), served as an indispensable midwife of almost all the industrial projects including the task of rounding out social overhead capital. Tasks charged to, and carried out (if falteringly) by, the Department included: To provide an institution for instruction in technology;[11] to supervise, and to manage, all the mines; to construct, and to repair, railroads, telegraph and light-houses; to build, and to repair, commercial- and war-ships; to survey land and sea; to process (refining and casting)

too. It may be noted that all these developments occurred several years before mechanical cotton spinning started the first stage of its real development, which came in 1887–90.

[11] The Technical School (Kogakuruo), established in August 1871 by the Depertmant, instituted a most strenuously intensive curriculum (eleven and one half hours scheduled class work every day) to develop native experts as rapidly as possible.

113

copper, iron and lead ores for use in various manufactures, and to engage in the construction of machines; etc. In discussing the ramifying development of social overhead capital in Meiji Japan, one probably should not fail to mention the energy and speed with which the public education system was instituted and made to spread in the early years of the Restoration. Coupled with the attempt to simplify the language and adapt it to modern technical needs as well, the early success of universal education in Japan was undoubtedly one of the most important factors in the rapid modernization of Japan.

Characteristsies of Japanese Capitalism in its Initial Stage: The Mechanism of 'Compound Interest'

7. A stroke of institutional transformation which changed the manner of disposal, if not the size, of the surplus was the Land Tax Reform of 1873 combined with the once-for-all step of commutation of feudal pensions.

During the latter-day years of the Tokugawa rule, it is estimated that the share of the feudal ruling class (lords and retainers) in the gross product of agriculture averaged around 37 per cent while the remainder was divided between land-owners and cultivators roughly in the proportion of 4 to 6. The Reform of 1873 was deliberate in freezing, at least initially, the relative ratios of distribution. The formula[12] was worked

[12] The formula for tenant-cultivated land was as follows:

$$L = \frac{rRP - (t + t')L}{i}$$

where L stands for land value, R for the quantity of rice crop, P for the unit price of rice, r for the percentage of rent to be paid in kind by tenants, t for the rate of land tax, t' for the rate of local surtax, and i for the conversion rate of interest. Originally both R and P were meant to be *current* figures. But they were frozen subsequently. All other parameters were given initially, $r = 68\%$, $t = 3\%$, $t' = 1\%$, out in such a way that 34 per cent of the gross product would go into government as tax, 34 per cent to the owner and 32 per cent to the tenant. The two significant innovations were (a) that the land value, instead of crop results, was made the basis of taxation to be paid by the landowner, and (b) that payment in kind, which was the practice under the feudal rule, was replaced by money payment, although tenants continued to pay the rent in kind. Now if the new central government had used the land tax revenue to support the livelihood of lords and retainers on a similar scale to that under the Tokugawa rule, the Restoration would have witnessed little change. What in fact was done was to transform the "status income" of the feudal ruling class into the form of transferrable assets, a kind of deadweight bonds unmatched by any productive efforts or physical assets, bearing interest of 7 to 10 per cent. 400,000 families were involved in this commutation step, the majority of whom received on average 400 yen worth of bonds.[13] For the period of 1868–80 as a whole, the land tax occupied 79 per cent of the central government revenue; and on the other hand, 42.1 per cent of government expenditures in 1878 consisted of interest payments.

8. The Land Tax Reform and the commutation of feudal pensions in themselves did not change the picture immediately. But their substantive contents, coupled with the progress of

and $i=4\%$, although t was reduced to 2.5% in 1877. Given the initial values of parameters, L becomes equal to 8.5 times RP. For the owner-cultivated land also, the formula and parametric values were chosen in such a way as to yield the same result of $L=8.5\ RP$.

[13] 500 of the so-called "lord class" received on average ¥60.000. One *koku* of rice cost ¥5.5 in 1877 and a family of four probably needed 4 *koku* of rice (¥22) simply to subsist a year, and even the 10% interest income on the principal of ¥400 would have been barely sufficient for minimum living.

inflation, had a tremendous leverage effect, which, of course, was not quite independent of policy intents of the Restoration leaders. Although it would be a mistake to attribute too much to these reforms, some of the major consequences related to them may be mentioned as follows:

(1) The Land Tax Reform perpetuated, for at least a generation more, the severe degree of exploitation in the feudal period of cultivating tenant-farmers. The rent-in-kind system made it certain that they would not benefit from any price rise of their crops.

(2) The land tax rate appeared to be rather exorbitant, taking away as much as one-third of the gross value of the crop; but it gradually lost its severity through the rise both in price and productivity of the rice crop.[14] Before this mitigation occurred, however, a large number of small-size landowners had suffered under the heavy burden of taxation and had had to sell their land to join the rank of tenant farmers; and relatively big landowners, who managed to survive the period of severity, came to enjoy a large surplus in the subsequent period.

(3) Many of the erstwhile feudal pensioners found income from the commutation bonds too meagre for their living even before the inflation came. But the inflation of 1877–81 had a crushing effect on them, forcing them to sell their bonds and to seek employment somewhere. With the progress in

---

[14] The tax, as mentioned earlier, was a flat rate on the frozen value of land to be paid in money. As the price of rice rose and/or the productivity rose, the tax became a smaller and smaller proportion of the gross value of the crop. By 1878, when inflation was in progress, the proportion of the tax in the gross value, which originally stood at 34 per cent, came down to 12 per cent.

inflation, the burden of interest payment on the government coffers also became smaller and smaller.

(4)   Government made use of the land tax revenue as a base for issuing various types of bonds, including industrial bonds. Thus while taking care of the expenses incurred on account of the compromise with the old regime, the Meiji government was able to channel some of the surplus directly into productive investment as well as to resort to deficit financing for creating new industries.

(5)   As the land tax had to be paid in money instead of in kind, the money economy spread rapidly in the rural sector of the economy as well.   At the same time, the revision of the National Bank Act in 1876, which permitted National Banks to issue their notes with the Commutation Bonds as collateral, created an attractive outlet for the holder of these bonds; and it stimulated the emergence of National Banks everywhere, causing the instrument for commuting feudal pensions to function as capital to spread the network of the banking system throughout the country.   In June 1876 there were only 4 National Banks; but three years later there were 139.

Here, then, are the trends and consequences of the Land Tax Reform and the commutation of feudal claims to income occurring, though with different timing and speed, in the years roughly from 1873 to 1881.   The inflation of 1877–81, which itself was partly a consequence of the measures associated with the commutation, helped to sharpen the process in the direction in which the events were moving. The most important of the trends, it may be said, was the income-redistribution effect and the polarization consequent on the Land Tax Reform, etc., creating on the one hand a large number of dispossessed peasants and former retainers and on the other a class of increasingly rich landowners and merchants. The government, which shared in the surplus, had an enlightened, energetic policy of channelling the surplus into productive investment, first under their direct ownership and supervision and then shifting to the policy of encouraging private enterprise, even if monopolies, with appropriate subsidies. The Mastukata deflation of 1881–85 was the period when all these trends and factors conspired to unite in preparing the ground for a rapid industrial development in the following decade.

9. At the risk of oversimplification, the essential features of Japan's "compound interest" mechanism in the last quarter of the nineteenth century may be skeletonized as follows:

Producers in the agricultural sector constituted the Atlas on which the severest bruden fell. Even with the rise in physical produtivity of rice and the diversification of typical products by an average peasant, including the ever-expanding industry of cocoon-raising, the lot of the majority of the rural population remained the same. Their added productivity expressed itself either in a greater surplus garnered by landowners and merchants *or* in relatively lower prices for the products.

The continuing plight of poor peasants contributed to cause an extremely low supply price for factory labour force, especially the type of labour force which the leading manufacturing industry of the time, i.e. cotton textiles, required. Young girls before marriage were recruited from destitute farm areas often in the form of contract labour in which parents were paid a nominal lump sum. Even in cases where the offer of labour for factory work was "voluntary", the supply price depended largely on the consideration of *supplementing* the family income and not much more.   It might be said that the survival of traditional family relations in Japan, encouraged for the interest of those who benefited from cheap labour, retarded the emergence of the category of wage income as a payment for principal breadwinners.   And it was only natural that the low wage rate in one important sector of the economy became the standard for other sectors and tended to pull down wages of all the alternative employment.

Being able to utilize excessively cheap labour force, new manufacturing industries of Japan could easily overcome various handicaps (such as the lack of tariff autonomy, the almost complete dependence on foreign supply of machinery, etc.) to establish themselves quickly with a high rate of profit.   With their profit earnings high, Japan's manufacturing firms became geared to a high rate of growth, supplementing their internal saving and sale of equities by heavily depending on commercial banks even for risk capital.   The *zaibatsu* structure of firms in Japan, which developed quite early, helped spread the risk over a wide range of capitalistic pursuits, a single *zaibatsu* organization encompassing practically all the major new industries as well as banking, warehousing, insurance, shipping and foreign commerce.

To the extent that the economy was geared to a high growth rate, the investment demand was high and took care of a significant portion of effective demand needed for the sustained prosperity.   But even so, the expansion of markets was imperative for products of new manufacturing industry, in particular, cotton textiles.   In general, the low income condition of peasants and workers precluded the creation of a mass market;

119

and the drive for exports was the natural consequence.[15] Japan's exports at that time were aided by (a) a deliberate policy of dumping,[16] (b) a fortuitous circumstance of silver depreciation, and (c) the expansionist military policy towards the continent of Asia. This latter expansionist orientation assured another sector of markets for Japanese industries, namely, the arms and arms-related industries which had a sheltered existence as regards not only the guarantee of sale with profit but also the supply of needed funds.

10. It cannot be doubted that cotton manufacturing was a leading industrial sector in Japan's take-off as Rostow points out. But it is questionable if the rapid growth of cotton manufacturing could be said to have been "a powerful and essential engine of economic transformation". (p. 58) I believe that the foregoing analysis points up sufficiently the complexity of the problem if we were to pin down such an "engine of

[15] Rostow states that "an environment of rising real incomes in agriculture, rooted in increased productivity, may be an important stimulus to new modern industrial sectors essential to the take-off." (p. 23.) Japan's case does not seem to support this thesis although he applies it to Japan. (See p. 67.) The first task the Japanese cotton textile industry was confronted with was to replace the British and other foreign imports within Japan; and while this was only half way done, it started an energetic move to drive a wedge in the world market. After only a few years of initial expansion of 1886–89, the mechanized spinning industry found itself with an unsold stock of cotton yarns and the industry had to agree on curtailment of operation for three months in 1890 when there were in existence only 278,000 spindles. The first attempt to find an export market for cotton yarns was also made in 1890.

[16] For example, the average price of cotton yarns per *kori* moved as follows: (Source: Koda Yudo, *Hompo Mengyo no Tokeiteki Kenkyu*, pp. 32–3)

	Average price at home	Average export price
1890	¥ 83.00	¥ 21.89
1891	73.00	71.31
1892	76.00	7.33
1893	82.00	5.01

transformation". Instead, I am rather inclined to see in the fact of the rapid growth of cotton manufacturing in Japan the developments which I believe are typical of the take-off period in a large number of countries: namely, the rise of joint stock companies and the prevalent use of machinery in factory production. The former facilitates the pooling of scattered savings in the economy for concentrated use in risk enterprises, and the latter renders production relatively independent of limitations of organic growth and permits cumulative mass production.

In the case of Japan, the stock market became an established institution in 1878; but initially their business was mainly the handling of government bonds. In 1879, for instance, the turnover of corporate shares amounted only to 1 per cent of that of government bonds. Such a ratio, however, rose to 13 per cent in 1885, then to 85 in 1886, and to 10,900 in 1887. The total amount of authorised capital in non-financial corporations increased from 13.4 million yen in 1884 to 189.4 million yen in 1890; and cotton manufacturing and railroads were by far the biggest industries which shared in this phenomenal multiplication of the corporate form of enterprise.

On the question of the supply of machinery, Japanese producers made full use of the flexibility of supply of foreign makers while at the same time taking active steps towards learning how to make it themselves. The lack of any inhibition in the purchase of foreign products in this regard, backed up of course by the availability of foreign exchange, made it possible for Japan's cotton manufacturing industry to expand as rapidly as investment funds were forthcoming. Average annual importation of spinning machinery, for example, amounted to ¥56,000 during 1883–86; but it rose to ¥125,000 in 1887, then jumped to ¥1,110,000 in 1888, and after a few years' stagnation it picked up again to reach the level of ¥5,402,000 by 1897. It is obvious that if Japan had been mindful of attaining self-sufficiency in machine-making too soon she would not have been able to expand cotton manufacturing as rapidly as she did. On the other hand, it is also evident that the pressure to expand Japan's exports—the pressure which had already been felt on account of the narrow domestic market—became all the stronger because of the need for sufficient foreign exchange. Were it not for the victory in the Sino-Japanese War (1894–95), which brought her the windfall of gold and sterling (364 million yen) as indemnity and which also opened a way for importation of foreign capital for the first time on any significant scale, it clearly would not have been possible for Japan to incur the aggregate unfavourable balance in commodity trade on the scale of 310 million yen over 1896–1900 and yet to take steps to join the camp of gold standard countries in 1897. Successful and successive wars, too, may be said to have been an important factor in the rapid industrialisation of Japan.

Chapter 8

ECONOMIC ASPECTS OF POST-WAR DEMOCRATIZATION IN JAPAN

[1960]

This essay was originally written as a contribution to the symposium planned by UNESCO for their *International Social Science Journal*, Volume 13, No. 1, 1961. This may be read as a sequel to Chapter 4, "Internal Industrial and Business Trends," of the author's earlier volume, *Essays on Japanese Economy*, 1958, No. 2 of the Institute publication series in English.

Introduction

Somehow the discipline of economics seems to have the habit of producing intermittent fashions which all but engulf the entire profession. As we enter the 1960s, the dominant fashion is 'growth economics'. Doubtless this concern with 'growth' everywhere, whether developed or underdeveloped, is rooted in the context of international politics today. Peaceful competition between rival social systems is visualized in terms of the rate of economic growth a country achieves or maintains; and there is an unending stream of books comparing the United States of America with the Union of Soviet Socialist Republics and India with China in this connexion. Technically minded economists, too, who generally deal with exteremely abstract models which appear to transcend institutional differences, have not escaped contamination by the 'growth economics' fever.

Against this general background it is interesting to note that the problem of economic democratization has again come up as a relevant issue impinging upon the growth performance of an economy. On the one hand, it is suggested[1] that a rapid rate of economic growth, which implies the successful functioning of an economy in the rational allocation of resources, is likely to be aided greatly by strengthening the economy's competitive mechanism through the break-up of monopolies, etc. The cases of West Germany and Japan, both of which have recorded a remarkable rate of growth even after the end of what could be regarded as the post-war rehabilitation period, are cited in support of this hypothesis. On the other hand, it has been contended, especially in Japan,[2] that certain hindrances to economic democratization such as the non-competing dual structure in the labour market and the economically irrational inequality of income distribution can and will best be removed automatically *if* the economy succeeds in maintaining a high rate of growth. In both respects, Japan's case is at issue; and what follows, it is hoped, will throw some light on these controversies also.

---

[1] See Egon Sohmen, 'Competition and Growth: The Lesson of West Germany', *The American Economic Review*, December 1959, pp. 986–1003.

[2] See, in particular, Hayato Ikeda in *Asahi Journal*, 2 August 1959, commenting on my article in the same journal two issues earlier.

The Break-up of Monopolies

It appears to be commonly believed that a most important measure of economic democratization in post-war Japan has been the breaking up of monopoly structures, called *zaibatsu*, which were pictured as basically family-controlled combines with an octopus-like hold over varied sectors of economic activity. The facts, however, are not so simple. In the initial period of the Allied Occupation, the problem of the *zaibatsu* presented itself less as a question of hindrance to democratization or to rational allocation of resources than as a moral issue, the *zaibatsu* having presumably worked hand in glove with the militarists in an unholy alliance to conquer the world. The Occupation policy was originally oriented towards keeping Japan's standard of living below that of any of the countries which she had invaded and to this end the dismantling of industrial equipment to be transferred to victim nations was undertaken as a measure of reparation. Even when the Far Eastern Commission in April 1947 raised the 'permissible' standard of living of Japanese to their 1930–34 level,[3] the restrictive element remained and thus it was only natural that pro and con discussions on the *zaibatsu* dissolution could not be conducted openly with reference to its relevance to economic efficiency. If the nation's standard of living was to be artificially restricted to a level below its own potential, the matter of attaining maximum economic efficiency could not be of prime consideration.

Practically all the anti-monopoly measures under the Oc-

---

[3] In real terms, it was probably about three times the level of the poorest victim nation in Asia and was approximately 30 per cent below Japan's 1960 level.

cupation were put into effect during this initial period, that is, before the end of 1947. The terms of reference were the directive, dated 6 September 1945, of the President of the United States which favoured 'a programme for the dissolution of the large industrial and banking combinations which have exercised control of a great part of Japan's trade and industry'.[4] First, the key holding companies at the apex of the *zaibatsu* structures were required to transfer their stocks to the Holding Company Liquidation Commission to be disposed of to the general public on the open market. This step was meant to strike at the head of the 'octopus' and to sever its 'legs'. Then came the Anti-Monopoly Law, incorporating, somewhat mechanically, many of the features of American antitrust legislation and designed to prevent the reappearance of any steps tending towards monopolies. A Fair Trade Commission was created under this law. The last of the measures was the Elimination of Excessive Concentration of Economic Power Law which passed the Diet, under strong pressure from the Occupation authorities, on 18 December 1947. The law, without setting up any clear-cut standards or criteria, conferred upon the Holding Company Liquidation Commission the authority to order the dissolution or reorganization of any corporation whose size or structure could be construed as having the character of 'excessive concentration of economic power.'

Change in Policy

It is quite conceivable that those in SCAP (Supreme Commander of the Allied Powers) who were technically in charge of

[4] Cf. T.A. Bisson, *Zaibatusu Dissolution in Japan*, Berkeley, University of California Press, 1954, p. 239.

carrying out these measures were genuinely desirous of promoting economic democratization in Japan in the sense of free and open competition which would facilitate free entry by newly aspiring entrepreneurs. But the manner in which these measures, especially the last, were hastily pushed down the throat of the reluctant Japanese, as well as the fact that they coincided with the lingering atmosphere of retributive justice, rendered their effective life much shorter than otherwise would have been the case. In particular, the SCAP policy on rehabilitating Japan's economy shifted somewhat abruptly in the early months of 1948. The turning point was indicated by the speech, on 6 January 1948, by Mr. K.C. Royall, United States Under-Secretary of the Army, in which he developed the thesis that, in the face of the new conditions in world politics, America's attitude towards Japan had to be re-examined and that these changes had produced 'an inevitable area of conflict between the original concept of broad demilitarization and the *new purpose* of building a self-supporting nation.' (Italics added.) The speech was rapidly followed by General McCoy's statement at the Far Eastern Commission (21 January 1948), the so-called Strike Report drafted for the United States Department of the Army by Overseas Consultants Incorporated (2 March 1948), and the Report of the Johnston Committee (19 May 1948) which concluded that the United States should, in its own interest, now assist in the industrial recovery of Japan. Once the tide was thus turned, any measure which appeared, or was alleged by the Japanese, to retard recovery was either watered down or suspended. The reparation target was drastically cut and the implementation of anti-monopoly legislation became entirely secondary to the need for utilizing the existing organization of industries to the fullest advantage. Few people considered whether cretain aspects, at least, of the anti-monopoly measures might not be of benefit to the long-term health of Japanese capitalism.

The fact that the anti-monopoly legislation was not voluntary on the part of the Japanese hastened the reversal process further. The Deconcentration Law was never seriously put into effect.[5] The Anti-Monopoly Law was soon revised to permit a manufacturing corporation to hold shares of competitive firms, to raise the upper limit of shareholding by financial institutions from 5 to 10 per cent, to legalize the system of interlocking directorates, and to widen the scope of cartels that could be formed. In view of the fact that enforcement of competition through prohibition of cartel agreements has been credited for the high growth-rate of the West German economy,[6] and also in view of the fact that pre-war Japan was characterized by an unusually large number of cartels, it is especially pertinent to inquire how far the post-war atmosphere of economic democratization succeeded in thwarting the revival of cartels. The fact of the matter is that even before the Anti-Monopoly Law, which prohibited cartels, was revised in 1953 to permit the formation of so-called 'depression cartels' and 'rationalization cartels', a number of *ad hoc* laws were passed to exempt specific industries under specific circumstances from the application of the Anti-Monopoly Law.[7] And even after the revision of this

[5] The Deconcentration Review Board, formed by SCAP and composed of five prominent businessmen from the United States, 'quickly found one reason or another to whittle down the number of corporations to be dissolved from 1,200 to 325, then to 30, then to 19, and finally when 9 corporations had been dissolved it announced that the deconcentration programme had been satisfactorily completed'. —K. Kawai, *Japan's American Interlude*, University of Chicago Press, 1960, p. 147.

[6] Cf. E. Sohmen, *op. cit.*, p. 994.

[7] Such, for example, as the Export Transaction Law of 1952 and the Interim Law for Stabilizing Specifically-designated Small and Medium Size Firms of 1952.

latter law, a series of interim laws came into existence covering such industries as coal-mining, textiles, machinery, electronics, ammonium sulphate, etc., to facilitate the formation of cartels still further. Ostensibly these interim laws were designed to enable the government office concerned to make use of an industry-wide organization for the purpose of co-ordinating the government plan for the industry with private enterprises in that industry. But it could hardly be denied that they had the effect of 'restraining trade' in favour of the strong existing firms. According to the *Annual Report of the Fair Trade Commission, 1957,* there were 41 major cartel agreements covering 22 industries in 1957 and semi-open cartels could be observed in 11 additional industries, without counting any of the 'invisible' cartels.

'Back to Normalcy'?

It was only natural that the 'back to normalcy' trend finally found its expression in the consolidation and realignment of firms along the former *zaibatsu* lines. Their trade names, such as Mitsui, Mitsubishi, Sumitomo, etc., which had once been barred from use, were revived after Japan regained its independence in 1952; and the forced separation and splintering of their erstwhile integral structures have been largely repaired. True, there are no longer holding companies at the apex which characteristically used to be controlled by *zaibatsu* families. In their place, however, has emerged the central role played by the bank of each group, such as the Mitsui Bank for the Mitsui group, and also a new co-ordinating organization of presidents of firms belonging to the same group.[8] The *Annual Report of the*

[8] Jugo-sha Kai, later renamed Itsuka Kai, for the Mitsui group (which also has a larger co-ordinating organization called Getsuyo Kai); Kin'yo Kai for the Mitsubishi group; and Hakusui Kai for the Sumitomo group.

Fair Trade Commission, 1957, summarizes the picture as follows:
'There can be observed a fairly marked trend to solidify
ties, through interpenetration of share ownership, among
the firms identified as belonging to the same *zaibatsu*
structure, such as Mitsui, Mitsubishi, Sumitomo, etc.
Percentages of shares owned by firms of the same group
are estimated to be 21.2 per cent in the Sumitomo group,
16.4 per cent in Mitsubishi and 11.0 per cent in Mitsui.
Considering the dispersion of ownership after the liquidation of holding companies, and further if we take into
account the additional shares under trust through investment trust devices, we may say that these percentages
indicate a safe enough margin for control by a given *zaibatsu*
group over the firms associated with it....It is especially
significant that more than half of such in-group share-
holdings are usually owned by financial institutions,
including banks, belonging to the same group. Since
they are able to exercise, over their financial counter, a
fair measure of control towards solidifying the group ties,
it could even be said that they are now taking the place
of former holding companies.'[9]

It would be rather far-fetched, however, simply to say that
the *zaibatsu* are returning. For one thing, the extra-economic
aspect of familial control over an elaborate combine, which used
to characterize the pre-war *zaibatsu*, is now definitely a thing of
the past. Even if a group bank, such as the Mitsui Bank, the
Mitsubishi Bank, etc., can be said, to some extent, to be taking
the place of the former *zaibatsu* holding company, it is doubtful
if it can ever attain the integrating and dominating power of

[9] Kosei Torihiki Iinkai (Fair Trade Commission), *Showa 32–nendo Nenji Hokoku*
(Annual report for the fiscal year 1957), p. 42.

the latter. Many big industrial firms of the *zaibatsu* type are increasingly attaining financial independence from the *zaibatsu*-associated bank through cumulative ploughing back of their earnings and diversified devices for financing their investment needs, including reliance on semi-governmental development banks. Furthermore, new industries stimulated by post-war technological innovations have tended to create new independent firms, as exemplified by the case of Sony Electronics Company. And after all, the Anti-Monopoly Law, which doubtless has been weakened through a series of revisions, is not entirely dead and can occasionally be invoked to come to the support of practices in the spirit of fair and vigorous competition.

However, just as it would be an exaggeration to say that *zaibatsu* are back on the scene, it can hardly be said that economic democratization in the sense of deconcentration has been successful. What we have is a new market structure, conditioned by various new factors in the situation, where both bigness and hierarchical ties exist, if at all, in a much more rational relation to each other than under the *zaibatsu* regime. Degrees of concentration within each industry, however measured, are at present essentially the same as in the pre-war period. And what has been especially characteristic of the Japanese market structure, namely the duality between modern big firms with high-wage workers and technically lagging small firms with subsistence-wage workers, remains essentially the same as before. This duality does not create two worlds independent of each other; actually the two sectors depend on each other, the big-firm sector often utilizing the small-firm sector as a cushion for the shocks of business fluctuations and usually as complementary shops for processing simpler parts. The dividing line between the two sectors is rarely crossed either

131

in relation to executives or workers. In this immobility, it may be claimed, lies a most important hindrance to the general goal of economic democratization in Japan. There is not only the obstacle to new entries created by large oligopolistic firms but also the various institutional practices which have developed to prevent mobility of the labour force across different firms and industries. Post-war economic development in Japan has not yet recorded any significant improvement in democratization as among firms. What then has been the picture in the sphere of labour relations and standards?

Labour Reforms under The Occupation

If the SCAP policy on democratization of the market structure could be said to have wavered between considerations of retributive justice and the genuine desire for the restoration of a competitive mechanism, the policy as regards labour reforms crystallized itself quite early in a set of measures which might be characterized as consistently 'New Deal'. The Japanese needed no prodding in carrying out these reforms.

Within a month after MacArthur's landing in Japan, political prisoners, including a large number of labour leaders, were ordered to be released; and in a matter of a few months the Trade Union Law, closely patterned after the United States Wagner Act of 1935, was passed in the Diet. The law safeguarded the right of labour to organize, to engage in collective bargaining, and to strike; and it further provided for labour relations boards at both the national and local levels to mediate in labour disputes. In 1946, the Labour Relations Adjustment Law came into existence, specifying the procedures for the grievance machinery at the disposal of workers. Major labour reform legislation was completed when the Labour Standards Law was passed in 1947, setting minimum standards for working hours, vacations, safety and sanitation safeguards, sick leave, accident compensation, restrictions on female and child labour, and other matters concerning workers' welfare.

This represented a possibility of evolving a modern, exemplary form of industrial relations—clearly a case of democracy by decree. More than a decade has elapsed since then; and judgement on the outcome must be somewhat mixed. The unionization of workers proceeded at a remarkable pace. While union membership in Japan, probably because of severe suppression, had never reached half a million at any time before the war, it went over the 5 million mark within a year after the passage of the Trade Union Law, and, with a slight dip at the time of the Korean War, has steadily increased to the 7 million level today. The ratio of organization now stands at over 35 per cent, actually higher than in the United States. Other labour reforms such as those relating to labour standards also took firm root at least in large modern establishments and are gradually encompassing a larger and larger sector of the economy. On the face of it the Occupation labour reforms appear generally to have been a success. In fact, they could even be said to have been an over-success. The momentum released by SCAP in this sphere actually went farther than SCAP had contemplated; and between 1947 and 1950 there were numerous occasions when SCAP had to take restraining measures to curb the excessive zeal manifested in Japan's trade union movement. The prohibition of the 1 February general strike in 1947, denial of union rights to government workers in 1948, revision of the Trade Union Law in 1949 to bring in the restrictive provisions of the Taft-Hartley Act, removal of trade union leaders from positions of influence in 1949, and the 'Red purge' of 1950 —these are some examples of the whip resorted to by SCAP and they show that the Japanese union movement was much more politically oriented than its American counterpart. And while the focus of attention was often this issue of success or over-success of labour reforms in terms of the standards which Americans have been accustomed to, one of the most important problems in democratization on Japan's labour front went relatively unheeded. That was the perennial problem of dual structure in employment associated with duality in employing firms.

Dual Structure in Employment

Conditions of democratization on the labour front, it might be suggested, should include (a) that the principle of 'equal pay for equal work' is generally applied, and (b) that an individual worker is free to choose his own calling and to apply at a place of his choice to be considered for employment without discrimination. When these conditions are satisfied, economic theory has it that rational allocation of labour resources will be achieved more or less automatically.

Japan, fortunately, has had no problem of discrimination in employment because of colour or religious belief. But the discriminatory and differential treatment of women used to be quite common in pre-war times. Furthermore another subtle discriminatory practice, whose cause lies deep-seated in the social tradition of the country, has characterized Japanese factory employment. The practice may be described in a somewhat schematic fashion as follows. Suppose we take the sector of manufacturing industries as our example. All the establishments in the sector can be divided, fairly distinctly, into two groups: large up-to-date firms on the one hand, and small technically backward firms on the other. The former recruits its workers from those recently graduated at a wage-rate not necessarily different from the one prevailing for new entrants anywhere. Once they are hired, however, they become 'permanent employees' of the establishment not to be dismissed or laid off until they reach retirement age. They become the core of the working force in a particular establishment and their grades and pay rise automatically with age. Since they may not be laid off even when business is slack, the management limits their number to the minimum and supplements them by a substantial number of temporary hands even in ordinary times. These in turn are of two kinds: (a) those who are usually hired for a period of more than a month and remain available as stand-bys for a particular firm even when not employed, and (b) those who are hired by the day. Even these arrangements may not be sufficient to meet the severity of fluctuations at times. Hence big firms usually acquire a fair number of small firms as sub-contractors. Workers in these small firms, whether they are directly associated with a big parent firm or not, are usually recruited nepotistically, sometimes from farms, sometimes from among older men, and sometimes from among recent graduates of the schools. In other words, the labour force in manufacturing can be divided into two clear groups: (a) permanent employees of big firms, and (b) others. It is most significant that there is practically no mobility between the two. It is also to be noted that, aside from the similarity in the starting wage, the wage-scale differs greatly between them. It is obvious that unless this duality is somehow done away with it cannot be said that democratization on the employment front has been achieved. What has been the record of the last 15 years?

The Crucial Test of Democratization

We must conclude that in spite of the favourable legislative progress, as well as continued awareness of the problem by many people, the duality on the employment front has not been broken. In fact, the remarkable progress in unionization has had the opposite effect, since unions have been mainly concerned with workers belonging to the 'permanent employees' of big firms. This fact, which could be substantiated more directly via detailed membership analysis of unions, might be gleaned from organization ratios of establishments classified by size. In the middle of 1956, the organization ratio of establishments employing 500 or more in manufacturing was 88.1 per cent, whereas it declined to 57.8 per cent in the category of establishments employing 100 to 499, to 20.2 per cent in the category of 30 to 99, and then to 2.9 per cent in the category employing less than 30.

At the risk of oversimplification we may surmise that out of the 7 million persons employed in manufacturing today, approximately 3 million, or 40 per cent, are in the favoured class of 'permanent employees' in relatively big establishments, i.e., those employing 100 or more, while the remainder is composed of either workers in small firms or 'stand-by' temporary workers in big firms. The organization ratio for this latter group of 4 million is estimated to be 7.2 per cent, and the impact of union activities on their lot is negligible. It is often contended that the vigorous union work of the favoured group tends to lift the wage scale of the non-favoured group. But careful analysis of the trend in wage differentials over the past decade seems to indicate actually the widening of the differential between the two groups. It is instructive to have a historical perspective on this question of wage differentials in Japan. In the early days of industrialization, i.e., at the turn of the century, the comparison of wage rates between workers in establishments employing 1,000 or more and those in establishments employing 5 to 9 indicated ratios of 100 to 80 for men and 100 to 75 for women. In the 1910s, the same comparison indicated a ratio of 100 to 70 for both sexes. In the post-second world war period, the ratio has fluctuated around 100 to 40. The focus may be placed on this latest period to observe a short-run change in such differentials. If we take the average cash earnings of workers in each year in manufacturing establishments employing 500 or more as 100, such earnings in establishments employing 30 to 99 stood at 67.3 in 1950, declined to 59.8 in 1953 and further declined to 56.1 in 1956. The Ministry of Labour warned, on the occasion of the publication of their latest detailed survey on wages on 8 May 1959, that wage differentials associated with the size of establishments had shown a further widening trend compared with the previous survey. For the sake of accuracy, in such an analysis of wage differentials, we must compare the wage rate of the same type of worker in terms of sex, age, and the number of years' experience in a certain skill with the sole difference being the type of establishment. The monumental research work carried out by the Ministry of Labour in 1954 enables us to do this; and the inference suggested above is found to be in no way altered. According to this study, for example, a male roller in a rolling mill, aged between 30 and 35 with 5 to 10 years' experience, would earn 100 in an establishment employing 1,000 or more but only 66 in an establishment employing 10 to 29.

It would be difficult to prove that union pressures in the area where workers are well organized have coincidentally had the effect of raising wages in the non-unionized sector. The fact of the matter may even be the reverse. And if such is the case, we have the paradoxical situation of organized workers in big firms sharing in the productivity rise with the monopoly capitalists who tend to exploit their subsidiary small firms which in turn can survive only by exploiting their non-union workers to the utmost. This is described as a paradoxical situation because the organized workers in big firms are the most radical element in Japanese politics while the unorganized workers in small firms have been shown generally to share the politically conservative views of their employers.[10] This paradox, however, is easily solved once we consider the sociology of the situation. The system of 'permanent employees' in modern big establishments has its roots in the patriarcal tradition of Japan, and the same can be said of the family-like atmosphere of small firms which inhibits the growth of trade unions requiring impersonal, matter-of-fact attitudes in support of individual rights. The duality in market structure, which may be said to have its economic logic in the given situation, goes hand in hand with the duality in employment structure which is a part of the sociological picture Japan presents today. None of the essential aspects of this situation can be independently dealt with. Thus the task of economic democratization, which no doubt involves only a part of the situation, has, in fact, to tackle the whole of it.

It can be shown without much difficulty that property income has declined relatively to the total of personal incomes in

[10] Cf. Shigeto Tsuru, *Keizai o Ugokasu Mono* (Forces behind economic dynamics), Tokyo, 1959, esp. pp. 68–75.

138

the course of the last quarter of a century,[11] and it may not be difficult to prove also that during the same span of time the size distribution of income in Japan has become more equal.   In this sense a measure of economic democratization has been achieved.   But on a most basic aspect of the task of democratization, i.e., to make the precept of 'equal pay for equal work' effective and to bring about the conditions for free mobility of labour, the post-war record has been less than satisfactory.   Difficult as the task may be, here is a challenge which Japan faces in the years to come.

[11] Ratios of personal rental income, of personal interest income, and of personal dividend income to the total of personal incomes were 9.7, 9.8 and 4.2 per cent respectively in 1934–36, but they were 1.8, 3.9 and 1.8 per cent respectively in 1958.

Chapter 9

EMPLOYMENT PROBLEMS IN JAPAN

[1960]

This essay originally formed a part of the Appendices of
a special report by a meeting of experts to the International
Labour Office on the subject of "Employment Objectives
in Economic Development" which was subsequently published by the same Office in 1961.   The author was a member of that meeting of experts.   It may be read as a sequel to
Chapter 5, "Employment in Japan," of the author's earlier
volume, *Essays on Japanese Economy*, 1958, No 2. of the
Institute publication series in English.

1.   Japan is not a newly industrialising country because it is
commonly aggreed that sustained economic growth in the
country began in the last quarter of the nineteenth century.
However, Japan does have a complex employment problem
today which in a number of respects is similar to that found in
other newly industrialising countries.   In the first place, the
agricultural sector is still beset with the problem of continuing
surplus labour resulting from technical progress and which is
not absorbed quickly enough in urban employment.   Then, the
proportion of employees in the total labour force is much smaller
than in most other industrialised countries, because a large

140

number of men and women are self-employed (individual proprietors) or are family workers. Lastly, it cannot be said that Japan's employment market is fully modernised since the employment policy of most firms is, even today, firmly based on the "permanent employee" system rooted in the sociological tradition of Japan—a system which helps to perpetuate the dual structure in employment and to weaken the healthy mobility of labour. This last point is probably the most important in Japan's efforts to modernise her employment market.

Dual Structure in Employment*

2. It might be suggested that modernisation of the employment market requires that (*a*) the precept of "equal pay for equal work" be generally practised, and that (*b*) an individual worker be free to choose his own calling and to apply at a place of his own choice to be considered for employment without discrimination. When these conditions are satisfied, economic theory has it that rational allocation of labour resources will be achieved more or less automatically.

3. Japan, fortunately, has had no problem of discrimination in employment due to colour or religion. But discriminatory and differential treatment of women was quite common before the Second World War. And, furthermore, there is yet another subtle discriminatory practice in Japanese factory employment, the cause of which must be sought in the social traditions of the country. This practice may be described in a somewhat schematic fashion. Let us take, as an example, the sector of

---

* This section reproduces more or less the section under the same heading in the previous chapter, pp. 134–8.

manufacturing industries. All the establishments in the sector can be divided into two fairly distinct groups: up-to-date large-scale firms on the one hand, and technically backward small firms on the other. The former recruit workers from new graduates of schools at a wage not necessarily different from that prevailing for new entrants anywhere. Once they are hired, however, they become permanent employees of the establishment and may not be dismissed or laid off until they reach retirement age. They become the core of the working force in an establishment and achieve promotion and higher pay as they become older. Since they are not to be laid off even when business is slack, the management limits their number to the minimum and, even under ordinary conditions, supplements the labour force by a substantial number of temporary hands. These in turn are of two kinds: (*a*) those who are usually hired for longer than a month and remain as stand-bys for a particular firm even when they are idle, and (*b*) those who are hired on a daily basis. Even these sources of temporary labour may not always be sufficient to meet severe fluctuations. Thus, big firms usually attract a fair number of small firms to which they contract out part of their work. Workers in these small firms, whether they are directly associated with a big parent firm or not, are usually recruited locally and/or nepotistically, either from farms, from among older men, or possibly from fresh graduates of schools. In other words, the labour force in manufacturing can be divided into two distinct groups; namely permanent employees of big firms, and others. It is most significant that there is practically no mobility between the two. It is also to be noted that, aside from the similarity in the starting wage, the wage scale differs widely between them.

4. The duality referred to has been the subject of discussion

for many years in Japan; and the problem of mitigating its undesirable effects, if not its dissolution, has been prominent in the process of democratisation in postwar Japan. There has been a definite improvement in the treatment of women workers, and it might have been thought that the mushroom growth of trade unions, coupled with the enlightened policy of the Government, would also have the effect of stimulating progress in the modernisation of the employment market. But achievements so far have been less than satisfactory. For one thing, the remarkable progress in unionisation has had an opposite effect, for unions have mainly affected the permanent employees of big firms. This fact, which could be substantiated by a detailed analysis of union membership, might be apparent from a study of organisation ratios of establishments classified by size. In the middle of 1956, the organisation ratio of establishments employing 500 or more in manufacturing was 88.1 per cent, whereas it dropped to 57.8 per cent for establishments employing 100 to 499, to 20.2 per cent for those employing between 30 and 99, and then to 2.9 per cent for those employing less than 30.

5. At the risk of over-simplification it may be estimated that out of the 7 million persons employed in manufacturing today approximately 3 million, or 40 per cent, are in the favoured class of permanent employees in relatively big establishments, i.e. those employing 100 or more, and that the remainder is composed either of workers in small firms or of "stand-by" temporary workers in big firms. The organisation ratio for this latter group of 4 million is estimated to be 7.2 per cent and the impact of union activities on their situation is truly negligible. It is often claimed that the vigorous union work of the favoured

group tends to raise the wage scale of the non-favoured group. But careful analysis of the trend in wage differentials over the past decade seems to indicate a widening of the differential between the two groups. It is interesting to consider this question of wage differentials in Japan from the historical point of view. In the early days of industrialisation, i.e. at the turn of the century, the comparison of wage rates between workers in establishments employing 1,000 or more and those in establishments employing five to nine indicated the ratios of 100 to 80 for men and 100 to 75 for women. In the decade 1910–20, such a comparison indicated the ratio of 100 to 70 for both sexes. But in the post-Second World War period, the ratio has fluctuated around 100 to 40. This latter period particularly shows a short-run change in such differentials. If we take the average cash earnings of workers in each year in manufacturing establishments employing 500 or more as 100, such earnings in establishments employing 30 to 99 stood at 67.3 in 1950, declined to 59.8 in 1953 and was further depressed to 56.1 in 1956. The Ministry of Labour warned, when publishing the latest detailed ministerial survey on wages on 8 May 1959, that the gap in wage differentails associated with the size of establishments had continued to increase since the previous survey. In such an analysis of wage differentials, for the sake of accuracy, the wage rate of the same type of worker in terms of sex, age, and the number of years of experience in a certain skill must be compared only with the difference in the type of establishment he is employed in. The monumental research work conducted by the Ministry of Labour in 1954 enables us to do this; and the inference suggested above is there confirmed. According to this study, for example, a male roller in a rolling mill aged between 30 and 35 with five to ten years' experience in the trade would earn 100 in an establishment employing 1,000 or more but only 66 in an establishment employing ten to 29.

6.   It will indeed be difficult to prove that union pressures in the area where workers are well organised have coincidentally had the effect of raising wages in the non-unionised sector. In fact, the reverse may well be the case.   And if this is so, here is a paradoxical situation of organised workers in big firms sharing in the productivity rise with the monopoly capitalists who tend to exploit their small subsidiary firms which, in turn, can survive only by exploiting their non-union workers to the utmost.

7.   This is a paradoxical sutuation, indeed, especially when it is remembered that the organised workers in big firms are the most radical element in Japanese politics while the unorganised workers in small firms have been shown generally to share the politically conservative views of their employers. The paradox, however, is resolved once we focus our attention on the sociology of the situation.   The system of permanent employees in big modern establishments has its roots in the patriarchal tradition of Japan, and the same can be said of the family-like atmsophere of small firms which inhibits the growth of trade unions requiring impersonal, matter-of-fact attitudes in defence of the individual rights of workers.   The duality in market structure, which may be said to have its economic justification in the fact that both the modern and the small firms depend on each other for survival, goes hand in hand with the duality in employment structure which is a part of the sociological picture in Japan today.   None of the essential aspects of this entire situation can be dealt with alone; and thus the task of modernising the employment market, though super-

ficially amenable to *ad hoc* measures directed simply to the purpose at hand, in fact unavoidably involves a whole range of problems where improvement will necessarily take time.

Absorption of Surplus Labour Force

Recent Experience

8.   The ratio of totally unemployed to the whole labour force, as estimated by the Labour Force Survey drawn up by the Statistics Bureau, has fluctuated between 1.2 and 1.5 per cent in the past ten years; and this fact seems to suggest that Japan has had no real unemployment problem.   But the definition of the term totally unemployed as used by the survey must be taken into account.   Here, totally unemployed includes "those who did not work at all during the one-week period covered by the monthly survey but were capable and willing to work and were actively seeking to find jobs, exclusive of those with employee status who did no work while receiving wages or those with proprietor status who did no work but whose family members or whose employees did some work."   Applying such a restrictive definition to the Japanese situation, the survey in fact minimises the unemployment problem in Japan and leaves outside the category of totally unemployed a large number of underemployed persons whose existence is characteristically related to the peculiarities of the Japanese society. The existence of underemployed may be briefly explained as follows:

(*a*)   the agricultural and forestry sector, which in recent years has accounted for between 35 and 40 per cent of the total labour force, clearly harbours today a sizeable amount of disguised unemployment;

(b)   even in the non-agricultural sector the category of individual proprietors and family workers, accounting for 20 and 12 per cent respectively of the total labour force in the sector, contains a fair amount of disguised unemployment, particularly in spheres where small shops over-compete with each other;

(c)   the section of the labour force made up of employees, which still accounts for less than one-half of the total, includes, as has been mentioned earlier, a large number of short-term and even less-favoured temporary workers.

9.   The task of making a numerical estimate of the underemployed in Japan is an extremely complex one, and is not attempted here.   But in appraising the record of absorption

TABLE 1

AVERAGE ANNUAL CHANGE IN LABOUR FORCE BY INDUSTRIES

(*In thousands*)

Occupational activity	1950–55[1]	1955–58[2]
Total	1,128	707
Unemployed	48	−40
Total gainfully occupied	1,080	747
Agriculture and forestry	−54	−463
Fisheries	−32	−3
Mining	4	3
Construction	110	90
Manufacturing	176	500
Commerce and finance	594	277
Transportation and communication	42	77
Services	326	247
Public servants	−50	20
Unclassified	−36	−3

[1]   Taken from S. Tsuru: *Essays on Japanese Economy* (Tokyo, 1958), p. 79.   [2]   Computed from a table in *Rodo Hakusho*, (Labour White Paper), 1959, published annually by the Ministry of Labour, pp. 258-9.   Newer series are based on the population of age 15 or higher whereas the earlier ones were based on the population of age 14 or higher.   Thus the two columns are not strictly comparable.

of the labour force in recent years, it will be essential to examine this zone of statistical twilight carefully to see how far the internal structure of the labour force has shifted in the direction of a more modernised and rational allocation of human resources.

10. The record during the past few years is rather encouraging in this respect. Table 1 gives the annual average changes in the labour force by industries over the two periods 1950–55 and 1955–58.

11. Whereas the earlier period was marked by an inordinate degree of absorption into "commerce and finance" and "services", the later period has witnessed the undoubtedly healthy sign of a rather drastic decline (463,000 per year) in "agriculture and forestry" which was more than compensated for by a significant increase (500,000 per year) in manufacturing.

12. An inspection of the trend in the composition of the labour force by status also gives an encouraging picture, as can be seen from table 2.

13. It is apparent from table 2 that the category of family workers is now definitely on the decline and that that of employees is surging ahead while the individual proprietors group is becoming stabilised.

TABLE 2

AVERAGE ANNUAL CHANGE IN LABOUR FORCE BY STATUS

(*In thousands*)

Status	1951–55	1955–58
Individual proprietors	188	47
Family workers	468	−370
Employees	598	1,090

Source: Calculated from *Rodo Hakusho*, 1959, *op. cit.*, p. 92.

14. It is of course dangerous to project, from such statistical evidence, that the trend will continue. Deeper analysis of
the factors underlying the recent changes is called for. But for
the moment we may make the following qualifying remarks:

(*a*) The total number of gainfully occupied in agriculture
and forestry, which was 14,888,000 in July 1959, still appears
to be excessive today. This number is slightly above that
of 1930 and the land-labour ratio has not shown any increase
over the last 30 years.

(*b*) There is unmistakable evidence that the relatively
largest gain in the sizeable absorption into manufacturing
in recent years was recorded in the smaller firms.[1]

(*c*) Although it is clear that the manufacturing sector did
the major absorbing job in recent years, especially in the form
of workers with employee status, it must be pointed out that
the category which swelled most was that of temporary
workers. Between 1955 and 1957, the rate of increase of
regularly employed workers in manufacturing was only 5
per cent whereas the similar rate for temporary workers
was 73.8 per cent; and out of the total increment in the
sector the increase of the latter accounted for 44.8 per cent.[2]

[1] Percentage increases of labour force in manufacturing classified by size of
firms and calculated for the two consecutive three-year periods are as follows:

	1951–54	1954–57
Total	%	%
	14.4	27.6
500 or more employees	7.1	15.3
100–499 employees	19.0	32.9
30–99 employees	20.7	38.9

Source: *Rodo Hakusho*, 1958, p. 37.

[2] Based on a survey of labour mobility carried out by the Ministry of Labour.
According to the definition used in this survey, "temporary workers" include
"regularly employed workers with temporary or day-labourer status" as defined
in the monthly labour survey by the same Ministry.

15. The generally encouraging picture of the recent period forms the background for the projection of supply and demand of labour attempted in the next section.

A Projection

16. Table 3 summarises a forecast by a government agency of the potential labour force during the next 20 years.

17. The estimates of population in table 3 can be presumed to be fairly accurate; but the projection on labour participation ratios is highly debatable.   It is true that the ratio had dropped 65.3 per cent by 1959; and that it can be assumed that the falling trend has continued.   But the factors underlying this trend are so complex that it is hard to tell what the net result will be.   The age composition of working population will be such that the relative declines in the age group 15–29 will be offset, by 1980, by the relative rise in age groups above 30; and differing participation rates of different age groups are likely to offset each other.   The inevitable rise in the standard of living and the improvement in the social security system, both of which will have the effect of lowering the participation

TABLE 3

SUPPLY OF LABOUR FORCE: A PROJECTION

(In thousands)

	1955[1]	1970	1980
Total population	89,270	102,210[2]	109,680[2]
Population aged 15 or higher	58,290	78,940[2]	83,940[2]
Labour force	39,910	49,770	50,070
Labour participation ratio	67.3%	63%[3]	59.7%[3]

[1] Actual census figures. [2] Estimated by the Institute of Population Research, Ministry of Welfare, 1 May 1957. The latest estimate (23 March 1960) has revised the 1980 figure of "population, aged 15 or higher" upwards by 2 million. [3] Projections by the Economic Planning Agency.

ratio, are easily predictable. But on the other hand, it is also likely that the modernisation of social customs will release the younger female generation from traditional domestic chores for office employment and that their participation ratio will rise. If the over-all participation ratio remains the same as in 1959, the supply of labour in 1970 will be higher by 2 million and that in 1980 by 6 million than the figures indicated in table 3.

18. There is another point worth special consideration. Although the average annual increase in labour supply between 1960 and 1970 is estimated to be around 850,000, the age composition of population today indicates clearly that the heaviest concentration of net increase will occur in the period between 1961 and 1966 when new additional jobs have to be found each year for more than 1 million people. This question of timing calls for a very forward-looking employment policy.

19. If we abstract from the problems attendant on shifts between industries and the peculiarly Japanese problem of duality referred to earlier, the task of attaining a balance between the demand and supply of employment can, of course, be solved by appropriate assumptions as regards the participa-

TABLE 4

PROJECTED ANNUAL PERCENTAGE RATES OF GROWTH

	1960–70	1970–80
Gross national product	7.0	5.0
Income produced in–		
Secondary industries	8.1	5.3
Tertiary industries	7.3	5.5
Per-man productivity in–		
Secondary industries	4.0	4.6
Tertiary industries	4.4	5.1

tion ratios, the rate of growth of the economy and the rise of productivity per man in different industries.

20. The Government's Economic Planning Agency has projected, for purposes not necessarily confined to the task of achieving a balance in the demand and supply of employment, relevant annual growth-rates as shown in table 4.

21. In the light of Japan's achievements during the last decade, these growth-rate projections may not be unrealistic. But bearing in mind the various extraordinary circumstances which have resulted in the remarkable performance of the Japanese economy in recent years,[3] it cannot just be assumed that the same trend will continue for a further decade or so. In particular, the projection of a 7 per cent annual growth rate for the coming decade, which implies the doubling of national income in ten years, is, to say the least, more optimistic than that given in the plans of most other countries.

TABLE 5

PROJECTION OF EMPLOYMENT TRENDS

(In thousands)

	1958[1]	1970[2]	1980[2]
Labour supply	43,680	49,770	50,070
Employment:			
Agricultural, forestry and fisheries	16,000	11,200	9,000
Mining, manufacturing and construction	11,200	16,700	17,800
Transportation, communication and public utilities	2,170	3,200	3,900
Services and others	13,750	18,700	19,300
Total	43,120	49,800	50,000

[1] Actual. [2] Projection.

[3] This entire problem calls for special treatment and is too complex to be even briefly discussed here.

152

22. The Economic Planning Agency further assumes that there will be a correlative association between the rate of decline in agricultural employment and the high rates of growth in other sectors of the economy, so that the coincidental changes in these rates during the period 1954–58 will continue. This is assuming a great deal; but the assumption could be a first approximation, and the over-all picture as given in table 5 ensues as a result.

23. This situation is based on a number of somewhat problematic assumptions. Will the participation ratio come down to as low as 60 per cent by 1980? Will the rate of growth of the economy be sustained at a high rate of 7 per cent for ten years, from 1960 to 1970? Will the shift of the labour force from agriculture to manufacturing be accomplished smoothly on the scale implied in this projection? These general questions no doubt have to be considered carefully; but probably far more important will be the problem of modernising the entire employment relations system in Japan in such a way that the adverse effects of the duality of employment structure will gradually disappear. It seems that the favourable turn of events of the past few years has led government planners to be satisfied more or less with an extrapolation of the relevant trends. But there is little doubt that if the projection shown in table 5 is to be realised, a set of clear and effective policy measures is now called for. Whether this can be achieved in view of the dominant trend of *laissez-faire* in the economic philosophy of present-day Japan is a problem which will become increasingly absorbing as the 1960s advance.

Chapter 10

GROWTH AND STABILITY OF THE POST-WAR JAPANESE ECONOMY

[1960]

This essay is based on the paper read at the annual meeting of the American Economic Association in December 1960 and was originally published in the *American Economic Review* (May 1961). In the light of what transpired during the past six years, the author does not feel any particular need for modifying the concluding paragraph of this essay.

Introduction

The postwar economy of Japan is characterized by an exceptionally high rate of growth, sustained thus far with little sign of retardation. Superficially, cyclical patterns are discernible; but they are in terms of changing values of positive rates of growth, even the smallest among them having been 3.7 per cent (in the year-to-year change of real gross national product). Looking behind the statistical indicators, furthermore, we find the impact on the economy of so many extraordinary and/or

154

noneconomic factors that we become wary of applying the tools of cyclical analysis to our subject matter. Thus the focus of this paper, partly for the reason of the limitation of space, is on the how and why of the high rate of growth which the Japanese economy appears to be maintaining, at least up to the end of 1960.

Summary of Statistical Indicators

With a view to giving a broad outline of the process of economic growth (and/or fluctuations) in the postwar Japan, Table 1 below summarizes some of the relevant statistical indicators in annual series and Table 2 presents annual rates of change in a selected number of series.

A number of salient points may be gleaned from these two tables:

1. Real GNP grew steadily over the entire period with little sign of retardation in the rate of growth. The picture of growth may be summarized by comparing three-year averages at the three points of time, as follows:

1946–48	100		100
1952–54	171	100	
1958–60		160	274
Average annual cumulative rate of growth	9.2%	8.2%	8.6%

The average rate of growth of 8.2 per cent between 1952–54 and 1958–60 can be said to be truly remarkable.[1]

2. Index of manufacturing production also presents a roughly similar picture except the early postwar years are more

[1] Between 1926 and 1939, a period of extraordinary expansion in the prewar Japan, such a rate was 4.6 per cent.

TABLE 1

MAJOR ECONOMIC INDICATORS IN POSTWAR JAPAN

Year	GNP[a] (real) (Billions of Yen)	GNP per Capita[b] (real) (1934–36 = 100)	Manufacturing Production Index[c] (1955 = 100)	Crude Index of Productivity in Manufacturing[d] (1955 = 100)	Commodity Exports[e] (Millions of Dollars)	Wholesale Price Index[f] (1934–36 = 1)	GDCF[g]/GNP	ΔGNP[h] Private Fixed Capital Investment	Special Procurement[i] Gross Receipts from Abroad on Goods and Services
1946	10.9	59	16.1	22.6	103	16.3	30.9%		
1947	13.0	68	20.1	33.2	174	48.2	32.6	91%	
1948	13.9	71	26.9	41.1	258	127.9	33.7	80	
1949	14.5	73	35.7	54.0	510	208.8	27.6	103	
1950	16.2	80	44.7		820	246.8	24.7		
1951	18.4	89	63.1	74.0	1,355	342.5	26.8	127	28.2%
1952	20.4	97	68.0	77.3	1,273	349.2	24.3	102	37.6
1953	21.7	102	84.2	91.7	1,275	351.6	25.8	70	36.9
1954	22.6	105	92.4	95.2	1,629	349.2	22.7	69	25.2
1955	24.9	114	100.0	100.0	2,011	343.0	25.1	75	20.8
1956	26.9	122	124.5	112.6	2,501	358.0	29.6	77	18.2
1957	28.8	130	146.4	119.4	2,858	368.8	30.0	50	15.1
1958	29.9	133	147.0	117.2	2,877	344.8	27.3	63	13.6
1959	35.0	154	185.0	136.4	3,457	348.3		67	11.3
1960	38.7	169							

a) Estimated by Economic Planning Agency and published in *Kokumin Shotoku Hakusho*, 1960, p. 192. The figure for 1959 is preliminary and the one for 1960 is an estimate on the basis of the preliminary figures up to the end of Oct., 1960. The series is expressed in terms of 1934–36 average prices and is for fiscal years beginning in April.

b) Based on the GNP figures in the table, divided by the population figures as of Oct. 1 for each year, and made into an index series by taking 1934–36 average as 100. Thus these are fiscal year figures also.

c) Constructed by the Ministry of International Trade and Industry. See the Bank of Japan, *Economic Statistics of Japan*, 1959, p. 2.

d) Obtained by dividing the index of manufacturing production in the table by the index, with the same base, of employment of regular workers in manufacturing. The latter index, constructed by the Ministry of Labor, is available for the years starting in 1951. (See *ibid.*, p. 289). For the earlier years, the Labor Force Survey figures for manufacturing by the Ministry of Labor were linked to the index by the author. The procedure admittedly is not very satisfactory.

e) Customs returns figures, published in *Tsusho Hakusho*, 1960, p. 568, for 1950–59, inclusive. For the earlier year figures, see Tsuru, *Essays on Japanese Economy*, p. 33. The single exchange rate of 360 yen to a dollar went into effect in Apr., 1949.

f) The Bank of Japan linked series. See the Bank of Japan, *op. cit.*, p. 269.

g) Estimated by Economic Planning Agency and published in *Kokumin Shotoku Hakusho*, 1960, p. 193. Fiscal year figures. Ratios are obtained by dividing the *real* gross domestic capital formation by the *real* GNP for each fiscal year.

h) Both terms in the ratio are real (1934–36 average prices) fiscal year figures each smoothed by taking three-year moving averages. Ratios are taken by lagging ΔGNP by one year. Original data are taken from *Kokumin Shotoku Hakusho*, 1960, p. 182, 192, and 198, except the figures for 1959 and 1960 are estimates by Osamu Shimomura in his paper read at the Meeting of Japanese Association of Theoretical Economics, Oct. 22, 1960, in Nagoya.

i) "Special procurement" is understood here in a broad sense and its annual series is taken from *Tsusho Hakusho*, 1960, p. 578. "Gross receipts from abroad on goods and services" is the sum of "Customs returns figures of exports" (f.o.b.), "Gross receipts on services, other than special procurement," and "Special procurement." See *ibid.*, pp. 568, 574–75.

157

patently characterized by the special process of recovery from the war-end nadir in industrial activities.

3. Per capita real GNP also grew steadily; but the prewar 1934–36 level was exceeded for the first time only in 1953.

4. The ratio of gross domestic capital formation to GNP fluctuated between 22.7 and 33.7 per cent and averaged 27.8 per cent over the years from 1946 to 1958, inclusive.

5. Excepting the three off-years of 1952, 1953, and 1958, commodity exports expanded generally at a remarkable rate. It has been estimated[2] that the elasticity of Japan's exports with respect to world income in the recent years has been 3 to 3.5; in other words, when world income rose by 4 per cent, Japan's exports rose by 12 to 14 per cent.

6. The level of wholesale prices rose more or less steadily, at an inflationary pitch, until 1951; but since then it has remained fairly stable, the 1959 level being 1.7 per cent above that of 1951. Meanwhile, the unit value index of exports declined by 22 per cent over the same period.

7. The annual rate of growth of real GNP presents a cyclical pattern, registering the low point of less than 4 per cent in 1948–49, 1953–54, and 1957–58. At the latter two points, the wholesale price index also turned downward. The slump in exports appears to be associated, with a lead, with the decline in the rate of growth of real GNP.

Our problem is first to acquaint ourselves with certain historical background of the period and then to attempt an explanation for the pattern of growth summarized above.

---

[2] By Dr. O. Shimomura. See his paper read at the meeting of the Japanese Association of Theoretical Economics, Oct. 22, 1960, in Nagoya, Japan.

TABLE 2

ANNUAL RATES OF CHANGE IN MAJOR ECOOMIC INDICATORS IN POSTWAR JAPAN[a]

Year	GNP (Real)	Manufacturing Production Index	Crude Index of Productivity in Manufacturing	Cash Earnings of Regular Workers in Manufacturing (Real)[b]	Commodity Exports
1946-47	19.2 %	24.9 %	46.9%	42.0%	68.7%
1947-48	7.4	33.8	23.8	25.0	48.2
1948-49	3.9	32.7	31.4	28.3	94.1
1949-50	12.2	25.2			60.7
1950-51	13.5	41.1	37.1	6.2	65.3
1951-52	10.5	7.8	4.5	11.2	−6.1
1952-53	6.7	23.8	18.6	5.1	0.2
1953-54	3.9	9.7	3.8	−0.9	27.8
1954-55	10.1	8.2	5.0	4.9	23.5
1955-56	8.2	23.5	12.6	8.9	24.4
1956-57	7.1	18.5	6.0	0.4	14.3
1957-58	3.7	0.4	−1.8	3.2	0.7
1958-59	17.0	25.9	16.4	7.3	20.2
1959-60	10.6				

a) Except the column on "cash earnings of regular workers in manufacturing," all the rates of changes are calculated from the figures in Table 1.

b) The figures for 1959-52 to 1958-59, inclusive, are calculated from the statistics given in the Bank of Japan, *Economic Statistics of Japan, 1959*, p. 289. The figures for the earlier years were estimated by the author on the basis of statistics in Tsuru, *Business Cycles in Post-War Japan* (1953) and linked to the series for the fifties. It should be possible to improve upon the figures for the earlier years.

159

Certain Historical Background

1. *Abnormalities.* Japan surrendered on August 15, 1945; and at least roughly for the subsequent four years her economy was in an extremely abnormal condition.[3] Abnormalities consisted of: (1) the process of rehabilitation from the nadir of defeat in a major war—the nadir characterized by the loss of one-fourth of the reproducible physical wealth and by the extreme slump in productive activities, less than 20 per cent in industrial production as a whole, and about 60 per cent in agricultural production, both compared with the 1934–36 averages; (2) the inflation of substantial magnitude, continuing unmitigated until the first quarter of 1949, with an accompanying phenomenon of widespread black and grey market prices in both consumers' and producers' goods; (3) the overriding influence of noneconomic policy decisions by the Occupation authorities on the economic life of the country—the policy decisions which were at first oriented towards restricting the tempo of recovery and then in early 1948 were rather abruptly turned in the opposite direction; and (4) the existence of all kinds of rigidities, either of deliberate or unavoidable character, which made the functioning of the market and price mechanisms extremely inept.

While these abnormalities lasted, it seems obvious that we cannot expect the Japanese economy to exhibit a process of economic fluctuation to which a technique of normal business cycle analysis can profitably be applied.

2. *When Did the Abnormalities Disappear?* When, then, did

[3] See S. Tsuru, *Business Cycles in Postwar Japan* (Tokyo: Science Council of Japan, 1953).

these abnormalities disappear from the scene? The answer depends somewhat on the nature of the problem we are interested in. If our concern is to account for a remarkable rate of sustained growth, we would need to know when the process of post-defeat rehabilitation can be said to have ended. On the other hand, if we are interested in the character of business cycles in postwar Japan, the fact that the country was, let us say, in the tail-end of the rehabilitation process need not necessarily discourage us from applying our tools of business cycle analysis. However, even when the nature of our problem is clearly set, it is not possible, I believe, unequivocally to date the point of time for the end of the rehabilitation process. There can be a number of alternative answers, such as: (a) The year in which per capita real income regained the prewar normal level: 1953 if the average of 1934–36 is taken as "the prewar normal," but 1957 if either 1938 or 1939 is taken as "the prewar normal." (b) The year in which the major sector of the economy regained, in physical output, the level of the pre-surrender peak. (In 1956 the index of manufacturing production went over the pre-surrender peak of 1941 and 1944.) (c) The approximate year when the productivity of investment (the reciprocal of over-all marginal capital-output ratio) became normal, having more or less exhausted the possibility of utilizing the pre-existing unused capacities. (As can be seen in Table 1, its smoothed-out magnitude began settling down, in 1953, to what may be considered a more normal value of 60–70 per cent as contrasted to an erratically high value up to that year.) (d) The year in which the real per capita GNP crossed from below Japan's historical trend line. (If we assume 2.5 per cent rate of growth and choose the average of 1934–36 as our base, the estimated achievement of 1960 still falls short of the trend line approximately by 10 per cent.) The hypothesis, to explain Japan's remarkable record of growth in the fifties, will be no doubt affected by the choice we make of the alternative signposts for the end of the rehabilitation process as indicated above.

The second of the abnormalities mentioned above, i.e., the inflation of substantial magnitude, ended, for all practical purposes, by the first quarter of 1949, although the outbreak of the Korean war in June, 1950, gave Japan another inflationary push bigger than the contemporaneous price rises in other countries.

The third of the abnormalities, i.e., the impinging of Occupation policies on the economy, can be said to have lasted, in a general sense, until the Peace Treaty became effective in April, 1952. But since the Occupation authorities themselves, by the end of 1948, started taking the initiative in restoring in Japan the efficacy of price mechanism and the system of free enterprise in general, the abnormality referred to, which may have lingered on beyond 1949, was not of a disruptive character in the latter years. Even the abrupt termination of the GARRIOA aid (Government Aid for Relief and Rehabilitation in Occupied Areas)[4] in June, 1951, did not have any disruptive effect on the Japanese economy since the "special procurement" by the United Nations forces for the Korean campaign smoothed the transition.

The fourth of the abnormalities, i.e., the rigidities born of the extraordinary post-defeat disruption of the economy, is the most difficult from the point of view of dating its disappearance. It is clear that by nature of the case it did not disappear by one stroke. But a most significant turning point was the setting of

[4] In 1948, for example, the American aid amounted to about 8.2 per cent of Japan's national income, or 179 per cent of her commercial exports.

a single exchange standard in April, 1949, which had an effect of opening the hothouse window, as it were, to let the cold wind of international market forces come into Japan.[5] This step to make the exchange rate effective, co-ordinated simultaneously with the so-called "Dodge disinflation" measures which were carried out with the uncontestable authority of the Occupation administration, gradually brought an order into the market mechanism, rewarding the efficient and punishing the laggard through neutral forces of competition in the market. True, governmental controls of all kinds died hard on the one hand and monopolistic arrangements of various sorts came to be revived in due course of time on the other. But the hardship of "disinflation" was soon mitigated by the buoyant windfall of the Korean conflict; and Japan's private business world, it may be said, regained confidence in running its own affairs by the time a recession set in in 1953. Thus it will not be far from the mark if we say that the peculiarly post-defeat abnormalities in the market mechanism of Japan were more or less corrected by the time the recession of 1953–54 ended.

In view of the above discussion on the historical background, one may conclude that for the purpose of growth analysis the significant date to begin it will probably be around 1952–54 or later and that for the purpose of cyclical analysis the coverage of years might be extended a few years further back though certainly not beyond 1949.

[5] Until the single exchange standard was established in April, 1949, Japanese exports and imports were transacted externally at world market prices but internally at the prevailing Japanese domestic prices. This meant that there were specific implied ratios of exchange for each commodity, yen-cheap for export goods and yen-dear for import goods, such ratios having a very wide range of 100 yen to a dollar to 900 yen to a dollar.

Interpretation

1. *The Shift in Structure.* If our judgment is that the process of post-defeat rehabilitation ended for all practical purposes by 1953 or thereabouts, we are still called upon to explain an extremely high rate of growth of 8.2 per cent per annum in real GNP between the three-year average of 1952–54 and that of 1958–60. One possible, and partial, explanation is the sizable shift in the industrial structure of the economy from the low-productivity sectors to the high. One can gauge the possible order of magnitude of the effect of such a shift on the growth rate from a hypothetical example where the relative size of the labor force in the low-productivity sector, having one-half the productivity of the high,[6] shifts from 60 to 40 per cent in six years. Without any change in the total labor force or in the productivity of either sector, real GNP can grow by 2 per cent per annum in such a case. It cannot be denied that the Japanese economy experienced such a shift in recent years; but the maximum that can be accounted for by this factor did not most likely exceed two percentage points per annum. And in any case, such a shift would require the corresponding increase in capital investment.

2. *High Investment and Its Cause.* It is evident that the *sine qua non* of the high rate of growth in the period we are focusing on was the sustained rate of high productive investment; and naturally statistical evidence is not lacking in this regard. The problem is to single out, if possible, the driving force behind it. A detailed analysis of quarterly figures of private fixed invest-

---

[6] Such a disparity may sound somewhat extreme even for illustrative purposes; but it is quite realistic in the context of the present Japanese situation.

ment in major manufacturing sectors reveals that they were correlated much less either with the value of product-sales or with the rate of operation, both in the preceding quarter, than either with the profit after tax or negatively with the rate of interest, again both in the preceding quarter.[7] This seems to suggest that private investment in plant and equipment was either autonomous or more a function of the rate of profit than a variable responding to an acceleration mechanism. High marginal efficiency of capital under the condition of price stability appears to have been a central factor in the situation.

If that is the case, we are pushed back further to explain the condition of sustained high marginal efficiency of capital. And I offer here a hypothesis that this was based upon the process of Japan's catching up with her own productivity potential. At the time the single exchange standard was established in April, 1949, it is quite clear that the realized productivity of Japan's manufacturing sector then was far below its own potentiality, owing to the incomplete recovery in external economies and the malallocation of resources consequent to rigidities of all kinds. The period subsequent to 1949 witnessed the recovery in these respects as well as the rapid introduction[8] of the innovations from which Japan had been isolated for about ten years and yet which could be absorbed by Japanese engineers and skilled workers without much delay. In no other way could we explain the trebling of per-man productivity in manufacturing in ten years between 1949 and 1959.

[7] See Economic Planning Agency, "Setsubi Toshi to Keiki Hendo" (mimeo., 1959), p. 28. Average correlation coefficients for manufacturing as a whole during the period from 1952 to the second quarter of 1958 are: $+0.769$ with the rate of operation, $+0.287$ with the value of product-sales, $+0.931$ with the profit after tax, and -0.946 with the rate of interest.

[8] The purchase of new foreign patents and the introduction of new foreign technique in general were permitted only in 1950.

Now, productivity rise is absorbed either by a fall in the price, a rise in the real wage rate, and/or a rise in the rate of profit. What did actually happen? First, the domestic wholesale price level has remained remarkably stable since 1951. *Prima facie*, this means that the latter two factors shared the fruit of productivity rise. Since all the statistical indicators point to the fact of a distinct lag in the rise of the real wage rate, the favorable effect on profit income appears to be indisputable.[9]

The problem as regards the price level calls for a further scrutiny. Although the average wholesale price level remained more or less stable between 1951 and 1959, industry component indexes are characterized by divergent movements. Whereas domestic prices of textiles appear to have been affected by the international price trend and have moved downward, domestic prices of metals and machinery have shown a rising trend, especially after 1954, and furthermore seem to have been maintained, often independently of export prices, suggesting a widespread practice by the industry of the dual price policy. A direct study on the subject reveals this to have been the case;[10] and it is difficult to escape the conclusion that as regards many exportable commodities the monopolistic price policy was practised at home while export prices were accommodated to

[9] The average annual rate of change in the unit labor cost (the index of wage rate divided by the index of productivity) in manufacturing is estimated by the Japanese government to have been +0.9 per cent for the U.S.A. between 1953 and 1958 and +1.2 per cent for Western Germany for the same period whereas it was −1.8 per cent for Japan between 1953 and 1959. (See *Keizai Hakusho*, 1960, p. 314.)

[10] See, in particular, Hitoshi Misonou, "Jiyuka de Kakaku Taikei wa Do Kawaru ka," *Keizai Seminar*, Oct., 1960, pp. 58–61. The ratio of export price to domestic "official standard" wholesale price for steel bars, for example, has recently moved from 80 per cent (Mar., 1957) to 76 (Mar., 1958) to 96 (Mar., 1959) to 89 (July, 1960). The similar ratio for ammonium sulphate at the same dates as above was: 98, 83, 78, and 78 per cent, respectively.

the dictate of international competition.   Whether export prices were below cost or not is difficult to tell.   But in view of the fact that the 360–yen-to-a-dollar rate, set in April, 1949, was in harmony with the abnormally low productivity situation in Japan at that time, the catching-up process mentioned above must have kept Japanese industries at a competitive advantage under the given exchange rate and under the condition of lagging wage rise.   It appears to me more plausible to assume that the apparent stability of domestic wholesale prices under such conditions meant continuous reaping of monopolistic profit by a certain number of industries—the monopolistic profit which became the basis for high plough-back.

The catching-up process, however, has to come to an end some time.   If we take the view that the trend line of 2.5 per cent rate of growth in real per capita income starting from the average of 1934–36 indicates roughly the realistic potentiality of the Japanese economy, we can say that, assuming the continuation of a high rate of growth in the immediate future, the catching-up process is likely to be over in a few years' time and that from then on the investment requirement for incremental rise in real output will be more normal.

3.   *Sources of High Effective Demand.*   High level of productive investment, which in general had an autonomous character in the case of Japan, must have created the supply capacity without necessarily generating sufficient demand.   Thus our next problem will be to examine the sources of effective demand which apparently supported the high rate of growth.

First of all, the role of external demand has been of special importance both as regards the growth situation and the cyclical pattern of the development.   The cyclical aspect arises not only because of the effect of exports on over-all effective demand but also via the monetary policy which has been geared to preventing the balance of payments from going too far into the red. When industrial activities expand, demand for raw material imports naturally rises; and if exports do not keep pace with imports in such a circumstance, the monetary authority adopts a tight money policy aiming to discourage further expansion. In both 1954 (February) and 1957 (May), the turning poing more or less coincided with the effective application of such a monetary policy.

In terms of the growth situation, the Korean conflict and the subsequent maintenance of "special procurement" demand were a distinct boon. (See Table 1 for the proportion of "special procurement" to the gross total receipts from abroad on goods and services.) But probably more important was the favorable cost situation of Japanese manufacturing industries due to the catching-up process discussed above. So long as the real wage rate does not quite catch up with the recovered potentiality of Japan's manufacturing industries, her exports will enjoy this cost advantage under the given exchange rate fixed in 1949.

Second, a number of important shifts can be indicated as regards consumers' behavior in the postwar Japan. In particular, the land reform, a part of the Occupation democratization program, contributed to transforming the rural life from the one largely characterized by poverty-stricken tenants to the one dominantly of small landowners who came to constitute a significant part of domestic market. This transformation probably had a boosting effect on the over-all demand situation more in the period of 1949–52 than in the latest. Then the tremendous upsurge in the propensity to purchase consumer durables, coupled with the coincidental introduction of con-

168

sumers' credit in a number of new fields, is undoubtedly of major importance, especially in the last several years. It is to be noted that the fashion of consumer durables is having a doubled impact in Japan inasmuch as those of prewar vintage (refrigerators, vacuum cleaners, automobiles, etc.) and those of postwar (television, room-coolers, etc.) are converging on Japanese households at the same time. Trend of home builders to turn more and more towards nonflammable, more durable, and thus more expensive, types of houses, making use of the products of high-productivity heavy industries, has also the effect of increasing the construction expenditure per unit of residential need, as well as creating a large new demand for heavy industry products.

Third, investment expenditures, while having the capacity increasing effect on the one hand, are no less important as a source of effective demand. While the fixed investment up till about 1954 was characterized mainly by the rehabilitation investment and by scattered cases of modernization, the investment in plant and equipment since 1955 has had a distinct slant in the direction of innovational investment. Thus if we choose as peculiarly innovational the following six fields, electrical and electronic equipments, automobiles, plastics, petro-chemicals, synthetic fibres and the atomic power, and if we calculate the ratio of fixed investment in them to the total such investment in manufacturing as a whole, the ratio of 15.4 per cent in 1954 and 14.9 per cent in 1955 registers a rise, annually from 1956 to 1959, to 22.5, 27.8, 31.8, and 34.9 per cent.[11] Innovational investment in such fields cannot be fruitful unless more basic heavy-industry sectors of the economy are capable of supplying

[11] Based on a study by the Ministry of International Trade and Industry. The figure for 1959 is preliminary.

intermediate goods of needed high quality. This process of modernization, in such sectors as steel, chemicals, and heavy engineering industries, preceded the flowering of innovational investment and became accelerated, since 1956, as they found a greater and greater demand at home for their improved products. Thus "the complementarity effect of investment" (A. Hirschman) is clearly indicated here; and the sky-rocketing increase in private investment on plant and equipment in 1956 and 1957 and also in 1959 can be concretely traced to such an effect.

Finally, we may take a look at that major offset to deflationary gap: defense expenditures in peacetime. If they are substantial, they can help sustain the effective demand, but at the same time they will divert resources from otherwise feasible productive investment to the consumptive type of expenditures. In Japan's case in the fifties, the expenditure on defense, which was started on her own in 1950, was large enough, one might say, to assure a continuing stable market for heavy industries which were just then on their way to recovery but was not large enough to drain resources away from productive investment. The ratio of budget expenditures on defense to GNP was 0.5 per cent in 1950, rose to 2.0 per cent in 1952, and thereafter followed a declining trend to 1.1 per cent in 1959.

4. *Other Considerations.* In addition to the above considerations in explanation of Japan's high rate of growth in recent years, one should probably mention, also, two other factors of some importance. First, the flexibility of supply of labor force has thus far been quite satisfactory. In spite of the extremely low ratio of unemployment to labor force throughout the postwar period (the range of 0.7 to 1.5 per cent between 1947 and 1959), the volume of disguised unemployment is known to

have been quite high, and in fact there has not been any difficulty for industries until quite recently to find additional labor force, even of qualified type, needed for expansion. The fact that Japanese workers started, in the post-defeat period, from an extremely low real wage level must have helped a great deal in bringing about a labor supply function favorable to industries' needs. Even if the present high growth rate continues, the pressure of demand on labor market is not likely to be felt until 1967 or thereafter, inasmuch as the postwar concentration of child-births is expected to yield an exceptionally high net increase in labor force until 1966. Furthermore, if the labor market is really pressed, the peculiarly Japanese institutional barriers against labor mobility will no doubt weaken, and a situation favorable to more rational allocation of labor resources is likely to ensue.

Second, the role of the government cannot be abstracted from Japan's growth process in the fifties. Although the so-called "Dodge Line" of 1949 did introduce into the Japanese scene important elements of competitive framework (such as the single exchange standard, the orthodox monetary policy, the negative attitude on government investment in industries, the use of budget surplus for debt retirement, the strengthening of anti-monopoly measures, etc.), it was on the whole short-lived except as regards a few measures that could not easily be reversed. Especially after April, 1952, when Japan regained her independence, it will be difficult to regard Japan, as Mr. Egon Sohmen does,[12] as an example of an economy able to achieve a high rate of growth because of its competitive structure. Monopolistic practices came back early; and the govern-

---

[12] See Egon Sohmen, "Competition and Growth: West Germany," *American Economic Review*, Dec., 1959, especially p. 1001.

ment embarked on a gigantic industry-financing program through a number of governmental development corporations, as well as introducing numerous tax-exemption or tax-relief measures aimed at specific industries and investment programs. The legacy of wartime high tax rates, which take time for eventual relaxation, has helped the government to enjoy relatively ample financial resources; and the level of treasury investments and loans has lately been of the magnitude fully comparable to the total retained income of corporations. The government has made use of such resources quite effectively now for one industry and now for another, shifting the emphasis as the circumstances demanded. The extent of corporate tax relief, on the other hand, is indicated by the rising ratio of the tax-exempt portion of corporate gross profit to the retained income of corporations. While the denominator itself expanded, the ratio rose from 9 per cent in 1951 to 113 per cent in 1952, 152 in 1953, and 213 in 1954.[13] It appears to be certain that were it not for such a sharing of risk by the government several of the essential industries would not have achieved the level of investment that was recorded in the fifties.

Future Outlook

As we review Japan's process of growth in this manner, there is not much mystery in the exceptionally high rate that has been attained between 1952–54 and 1958–60. There remains, however, a question of the future. If my preceding analysis is correct, one important element in the situation, i.e., what I called the "catching-up process," is soon to become a negligible

[13] See Economic Planning Agency, *Sengo Nihon no Shihon Chikuseki to Kigyo Keiei*, 1957, p. 156.

factor. Even then, major shifts in production functions are yet to come in a number of industries, as well as the further shift upward in the demand for consumer durables. The prospect, therefore, is still the feasibility of continuing a fairly high rate of growth in the coming decade, with, however, the following qualifications: (1) that it is likely that a high growth rate will depend more and more on the demand situation than on the realized profit rate from now on; (2) that, in particular, the doubled efforts for the maintenance and expansion of Japan's export markets will be required; (3) that the social overhead structures, providing external economies for the private sector, will demand a greater share of the total capital needs in the future[14]; and (4) that it will become increasingly important to break the peculiarly Japanese institutional barriers against labor mobility.

Whether a high growth rate can be maintained with reasonable stability of the economy or whether a high growth rate, as such, will be able to solve various structural problems Japan suffers from[15] is, I believe, a different problem.

[14] The proportion of social overhead capital in the total reproducible physical wealth of Japan has been declining steadily since 1946; i.e., from 51.0 per cent in 1946 to 42.2 per cent in 1957. (See Economic Planning Agency, *Sengo Nihon no Keizai Seicho*, 1959, p. 12.)

[15] In particular, the problem of so-called "dual structure"; i.e., the coexistence of and the lack of labor mobility between the modern high-wage sector with large size on the one hand and the technically-lagging low-wage sector with small size on the other.

Chapter 11

ECONOMIC PLANNING AND PROGRAMMING
IN JAPAN

[1962]

This essay appeared originally in *Planning Economic Development*, 1963, edited by Everett E. Hagen, under the title of "Formal Planning Divorced from Action: Japan". No revision has been made on that version except that the bibliography there appended is omitted here for the reason that it was not prepared by the author himself.

There have been enough voluminous documents issued by the government on national planning in postwar Japan to fill a small room.   One can count more than a dozen separate plans in a brief period of fifteen years, each replacing its predecessor in the manner of Penelope's web.   None of them, however, can be called national planning in the real sense of the term. Each was a product of the times, reflecting the basic institutional orientation of the economy as well as the overriding issues of the day.

Planning under the Occupation, 1945–1952

The Policy of Economic Demilitarization

It was unavoidable that any economic planning or programming in Japan before her regaining of independence should be strongly circumscribed by the policy of the occupying authorities acting basically in accordance with the Potsdam Declaration of July 26, 1945, which defined the terms for Japanese surrender. Article XI of this document states: "Japan shall be permitted to maintain such industries as will sustain her economy and permit the exaction of just reparations in kind, but not those which would enable her to re-arm for war. To this end, access to, as distinguished from control of, raw materials shall be permitted. Eventual Japanese participation in world trade relations shall be permitted."

This statement was further amplified in relevant paragraphs of the United States "Initial Post-Surrender Policy for Japan" (September 22, 1945) which, *inter alia*, specified the policy directives of "the elimination in Japan of those selected industries or branches of production whose chief value to Japan is in preparing for war; the prohibition of specialized research and institutions directed to the development of war-making power; and the limitation of the size and character of Japan's heavy industries to its future peaceful requirements."

What these phrases meant, however, was not clear until the Pauley Reparations Mission issued its "Interim Reparations Program" on December 7, 1945. The severity of the occupation policy as regards economic matters was realized for the first time through the statement of E.W. Pauley on that occasion, which began with a brief paragraph: "Four years ago today Japan attacked Pearl Harbor. America will never forget the attack. Japan will never forget the consequences." He went on to say that: "The fact is that Japan's industrial equipment was overwhelmingly designed for war. Despite all the destruction, Japan still retains, in workable condition, more plant and equipment than its rulers ever allowed to be used for civilian supply and consumption even in peaceful years — — [For example] in steel, Japan's own figures show that she still has, in workable condition, more than twice the facilities that she had when she invaded Manchuria in 1931."[1]

The Interim Reparations Program recommended that out of the estimated steel capacity of 11,000,000 tons "all the working capacity in excess of 2,500,000[2] tons per year" should be removed and that half the capacity for the manufacture of machine tools should be taken out. The Interim Program was revised in the direction of broader coverage and severity in the final recommendation of the Pauley Mission issued in November 1946.

In order to determine "the excess capacity over peaceful needs" it was necessary to specify the quantitative level of "peaceful needs," The thinking of the occupying powers on this matter was not made clear until the Far Eastern Commission issued a policy decision on January 23, 1947, which stated: "The Far Eastern Commission determines as a matter of policy that the peaceful needs of the Japanese people should be defined as being substantially the standard of living prevailing in Japan during the period of 1930–1934. Data about the standard of

[1] SCAP, Public Relations Office, press release, December 7, 1945.
[2] By the end of 1961 Japan was producing more than this amount monthly.

176

living of 1930–1934 should for present purposes be used to make an estimate of Japan's peaceful needs in 1950."

Not knowing this policy decision in advance, several offices of the Japanese government began drafting, even before the Interim Reparations Program was made public, over-all plans for economic rehabilitation designed to point up specific needs and requirements for regaining the prewar standard of living within the framework of the United States Initial Post-Surrender Policy for Japan. When the Interim Reparations Program was made known, these studies found a new orientation of defensive character, that is, a new purpose of attempting to impress upon the Reparations Mission the need for retaining within Japan more of her industrial capacities than the Mission had recommended. For this purpose they were obliged to choose a base prewar year as the acceptable standard for peaceful existence and a future target year as a probable date to regain it. The years 1930 and 1950 were chosen as such dates. Of the several which could be counted among these studies, we might mention the following two as most significant: the "Foreign Office Projection," November 1946, and the "Supply Capacity Study Group Projection," November 1946.

Both projections, particularly the latter, bore the earmark of the wartime habit of thinking conditioned by the existence of detailed materials control and allocation. In other words, the projections were the demand for and supply of raw materials, involving the calculation of per capita needs of essential goods and of materials requirements per unit of output in major industries.[3] It is noteworthy that both projections assumed no foreign borrowing or aid in the process of Japan's regaining the 1930 standard of living by 1950. However, whereas the

[3] These are the so-called "technical coefficients."

Foreign Office Projection depicted the needs and requirements that were logically implied in this rehabilitation goal, the Supply Capacity Study Group Projection chose to show the year-to-year process of building up to the 1950 target from the conditions of 1945. Thus the latter had the merit of bringing into relief specific areas of important bottlenecks. It was through this study that the supply of coal was found to be the basic bottleneck and the top-priority plan for coal was launched by the government. At any rate, both projections, which were by accident made public almost simultaneously with the final recommendation of the Pauley Mission, played in effect the role of protest against the latter, attempting to show how difficult it would be for Japan to recover the 1930 level even without the handicap of reparations. This conclusion was strengthened when, two months later, the Far Eastern Commission defined "the peaceful needs of the Japanese people" to be "substantially the standard of living prevailing in Japan during the period of 1930–1934," inasmuch as this latter level was higher than that of 1930.

A New Policy Emphasizing Self-Support

The Allied policy of economic demilitarization, reparations, and restriction remained unchanged at least till the early summer of 1947, so far as we can judge from the general tone of the "Basic Post-Surrender Policy for Japan" issued by the Far Eastern Commission on June 19, 1947. But at some point of time between this date and January 1948 United States policy on Japan seems to have shifted from the line originally set forth in the Postdam Declaration. The Japanese government had the first inkling of a new trend when a new Reparations Mission, headed by Mr. Strike of Overseas Consultants,

178

Inc., arrived in Japan in January 1947, with the apparent intention of revising the Pauley recommendation. The Mission's second visit in August 1947 strengthened that impression, and the publication of their report in March 1948 confirmed it.

However, in advance of this latter date the official announcement of the shift had already been made public. On January 6, 1948, K.C. Royall, U.S. Under Secretary of the Army, spoke at San Francisco and developed the theme that America's attitude toward Japan had to be re-examined, since the new conditions in world politics had produced "an inevitable area of conflict betwen the original concept of broad demilitarization and the new purpose of building a self-supporting nation." He went on to say that: "At some stage extreme deconcentration of industry, while further impairing the ability to make war, may, at the same time, destroy manufacturing efficiency of Japanese industry—may, therefore, postpone the day when Japan can become self-supporting." The Royall speech was a significant point of departure which was rapidly followed by General McCoy's statement before the Far Eastern Commission (January 21, 1948), the Strike report mentioned earlier (March 2, 1948), and the report of the Johnston Committee (May 19, 1948), which concluded that the United States should, in its own interest, now assist in the industrial recovery of Japan.[4]

[4] The shift in reparations proposals is clearly indicated by the following figures (millions of yen in 1939 prices):

	Industrial Equipment	Military Equipment	Total
Pauley proposal	990	1,476	2,466
Strike proposal	172	1,476	1,648
Johnston proposal	102	560	662
Actual removal[a]			160

[a] The value of total actual removal before the removal was stopped in the spring of 1949. See *Ekonomisuto*, April 15, 1955, p. 72.

It was against this background that the Japanese government had started to turn a new leaf in economic planning.

In the first general election after the new Constitution was adopted the Socialist party won a plurality, and Mr. Katayama, a Socialist, headed the coalition Cabinet which was organized on June 1, 1947. As might be expected, the new government was highly "plan conscious," with its enlarged and revitalized Economic Stabilization Board (ESB) as its spearhead. The chief authors of two earlier projections (Foreign Office Projection and Supply Capacity Study Group Projection), Saburo Okita and Hidezo Inaba, now joined the staff of the ESB, and within this office the Secretariat for Long-Range Planning was established in July 1947. The herculean labor of this Secretariat produced a "Draft Plan for Economic Rehabilitation" in May 1948, by which time, however, the Katayama Cabinet had fallen and the spirit of reform had been greatly abated. At least, however, the draft plan received encouragement from the objective atmosphere of the new U.S. policy for Japan which was officially enunciated in January 1948.

The draft plan set the target of regaining the 1930–34 standard of living by 1952, by which time, it was proposed, Japan's external accounts would roughly balance and the number of unemployed would be reduced to a manageable proportion of about two million. It was suggested that in the process of attaining this target the industrial structure should become slanted more and more toward heavy and chemical industries and that outside aid to the tune of some $1.5 billion would be needed during the period 1948–51. These two conditions constituted radical innovation when contrasted to earlier plans and projections, changing the nature of a plan from defensive to positive. The main body of the draft plan itself was a detailed spelling out, year by year, of practically all aspects of the economy from the projection of population and labor-force changes, tables of supply of all the major intermediate products and final consumption goods, productivity changes, foreign trade prospects, and public finance, to social economic accounting.

It was indeed complete except for the most important element in such a plan: it failed to indicate how to go about implementing the plan. In a sense this failing was understandable inasmuch as the Japanese government at the time was still shackled with the occupation restrictions and, furthermore, the overriding problem then was that of controlling the intractable inflation. Authors of the draft plan were apparently under no illusion as to the incompleteness of their plan, since they stated in the concluding chapter that "the question of how to implement this plan is little discussed here and remains to be taken up in the future."[5] It appears that they were satisfied to show as realistically as possible the conditions and requirements for rehabilitation with a given speed in terms of both macroeconomic relations and detailed materials requirements. As such the draft plan had its positive historic significance.

Although encouraged by the new orientation of U.S. policy for Japan, the atmosphere in Japan in the middle of 1948 was far from optimistic. Industrial production, though slowly rising, was still hovering around the level of 60 per cent of

---

[5] They did indicate, however, in broad strokes, a few practical matters of implementation such as: (1) that a strong measure of government control was still needed inasmuch as in the disrupted condition of postwar markets the high profit rate did not necessarily coincide with high social desirability; (2) that government control should choose a limited area in which it could be concentrated in order that such control could be really effective; (3) that a few economic activities, such as new development of hydroelectric power and of coal mines, might be undertaken directly by the government itself; and so on.

1930–34; an inflationary price rise was continuing at the rate of more than 100 per cent per annum; and the degree of reliance on U.S. aid was as high as 8.2 per cent of Japan's national income in 1948. The prognosis of Dr. E.A. Ackerman, a member of General MacArthur's staff, written against the background of 1948 economic conditions, was shared by many an expert at that time:

> In the light of an analysis of its resources, the Japan of the next three decades appears likely to have one of two aspects if its population continues to grow to 100 million or more. (1) It may have a standard of living equivalent to that of 1930–34 if foreign financial assistance is continued indefinitely. (2) It may be "self-supporting," but with internal political, economic, and social distress and a standard of living gradually approaching the bare subsistence level. Either of these alternatives seems more likely than that of a Japan which will have made itself self-supporting at a 1930–34 standard through foreign trade and improved resources utilization.[6]

It was against this background that the Ashida Cabinet, though much less "plan conscious" than its predecessor, apparently felt the urgent need for planned rehabilitation efforts and set up in May 1948 an extensive organization, the Planning Commission for Economic Rehabilitation, headed by the Prime Minister himself. The earlier draft plan constituted a legacy on which the new Commission was to build up its own work. Naturally, a greater degree of realism was gained through further experience; and it was realized at the outset that implementation of any plan would have to wrestle with the immediate problem of inflation. Thus the plan period of 1949

[6] E.A. Ackerman, *Japanese Natural Resources* (Tokyo: GHQ, SCAP, NRS, 1949), p. 528.

to 1953 was divided into two subperiods: the first part, 1949–1950, to achieve economic stability, and the second part, 1951–1953, to attain economic viability, that is, the ability to carry on a full-employment level of economic activity without continuing foreign economic assistance.

This time again, however, external factors moved rapidly to discompose the Commission. The Commission as a whole was inclined toward the idea of combating inflation through redoubled efforts in increasing the supply of bottleneck commodities. But the occupation authorities apparently thought otherwise. The United States government sent the Young Mission to Japan in the early summer of 1948 in order to draw up a coordinated policy of anti-inflation. On the basis of the recommendation of the Mission the "Nine-Point Program" was issued in December 1948 in the form of a directive by General MacArthur to the Japanese government. The first of the nine points, which was apparently regarded as the most important, stated: "To achieve a true balance in the consolidated budget at the earliest possible date by stringent curtailing of expenditures and maximum expansion in total government revenues, including such new revenue as may be necessary and appropriate." In essence the Nine-Point Program was a program of rigorous deflation which, being a bitter pill, no political party was willing to sponsor. Responsibility for carrying it out had to rest on the power of the occupation. Joseph Dodge arrived in February 1949 to assume the role of unpopular surgeon. It was history's accident that Mr. Dodge's arrival coincided with the formation of the Yoshida Cabinet, the most conservative yet since surrender.

In retrospect it is quite clear that the philosophy of the Dodge stabilization program was the resuscitation of the efficacy of a price mechanism resting on free enterprise and effective competition; it was envisaged that the government's role and the influence of government policies on the pace and direction of economic development would be minimal. The philosophy could not easily be harmonized with the basic tenet of planning that had dominated the thinking of the Planning Commission for Economic Rehabilitation. Ruffled as many members were by the development of a new occupation policy, the Commission went on with its work, somehow adjusting itself to the Dodge program and completed its long report, the "Economic Rehabilitation Plan," toward the end of May 1949. As might have been expected, Prime Minister Yoshida was highly critical of the plan and suggested "recasting the whole thing with more international awareness." What he meant by "international awareness" was never made clear; but the Commission, slightly reorganized, spent the next few months in the work of dress-up revision. However, the spirit was no longer there and the salvaging operation was a failure. Finally in September 1949 it was decided to bury the plan, and Mr. Yoshida explained the reason in the Diet in October, saying that "long-range planning is meaningless."

Nevertheless, the "Economic Rehabilitation Plan" was a monument—a monument built on all the earlier plans and projections, initiating a countless number of new statistical studies and issuing 519 documents in the short span of a single year. Within the framework set by the desiderata of the plan, it was an eminently inductive study, pursuing to the minutest detail any matter of quantitative estimate. In other words, trees were finely delineated but the forest was not necessarily lost sight of. With keen awareness of the limitation of the Japanese politico-economic structure at the time, the plan proposed to limit the areas of leverage for planning to the following four: maximum effort to expand exports; emphasis on capital accumulation and the rational channeling of investment funds; strong measures to limit population growth; and the retention, after streamlining, of effective governmental control. Each one of these points was further detailed; and with little trace of optimism, understandably so in the atmosphere of 1948–49, the plan concluded its report by appealing to the Japanese people for further sacrifice and redoubled efforts.

Effects of the Korean War

As it turned out, the projection of the Economic Rehabilitation Plan would have been fairly realistic but for the windfall of the Korean War prosperity.[7] In support of such judgment one might contrast the projected level of exports with the actual achievements, without including "special procurements" which were directly due to the Korean War, as in Table 1. The total for the five years is about the same, but the actual achievement in 1953 fell short of the target by some 13 per cent. "Special procurements," on the other hand, were as high as 44, 65, and 63 per cent, respectively, of commercial exports in 1951, 1952, and 1953; and they played the double role of boosting

[7] For some of the important items, the contrast between the projection and the actual achievement for 1953 was as folllws:

	Index of Manufacturing and Mining Production (1930–34=100)	Exports (Millions of Dollars in 1953 Prices)	Per Capita Real Income (1930–34=100)
Projection	68.3	1,511	89.9
Actual	85.7	2,084a)	110.1

a) Includes "special procurements" by the U.S. government to the amount of $809 million.

TABLE 1

CommerciaL Exports

(Millions of dollars in 1953 prices)

	Projection	Actual
1949	578	493
1950	760	985
1951	965	1,112
1952	1,211	1,178
1953	1,458	1,275

Note: "Projection" refers to fiscal years which begin on April 1 of the year indicated; "actual" refers to calendar years. (This difference is not very important for the present purpose.) Both series are expressed in constant 1953 dollars by using the export unit value index compiled by the Bank of Japan.

effective demand and earning enough dollars for needed imports. This fortuitous conjuncture, coupled with the laissez faire atmosphere of the Dodge stabilization program, which laid emphasis on orthodox monetary policy, provided no encouragement for economic planning. Furthermore, Prime Minister Yoshida's dislike for planning of any sort made it certain that the ghost of the ertswhile Planning Commission would not be revived.

Yoshida continued in office until December 1954, when his Cabinet was dislodged by a vote of nonconfidence in the Diet. So long as he was at the helm it was not possible to draw up an over-all plan or projection of the type which he himself buried in 1949. But before Japan regained her independence in April 1952, through the coming into effect of the peace treaty, there appeared a number of governmental studies which could be classified under the broad category of planning and projection. These studies both reflected the need of the times and constituted a way of asserting, on the part of planning-oriented officials in

186

the government, the *raison d'être* of their own office. Three of them are mentioned here:

1. Conditions for Achieving Economic Self-Support, or "Eos Study."
2. Economic Self-Support Plan.
3. Document B.

The Eos Study, so named with a hope of dawn, was made public in June 1950, only a few weeks before the Korean conflict began. It was drafted largely in response to Mr. Dodge's critical remark to the effect that Japan should work toward freeing herself as quickly as possible from the artificial aid of the U.S. government. The Economic Rehabilitation Plan of 1949 could be criticized for having been somewhat easy-going in its assumption of continuing U.S. aid. By 1950 Japanese planners realized that the U.S. attitude might be more severe than they had expected. They hurriedly adjusted the figures of earlier studies to give specific answers to three problems considered urgent: how to expedite the export drive needed for attaining economic viability by 1952; how to meet the crisis of a dollar shortage if and when U.S. aid were suddenly discontinued; and how to fill the gap in investment funds when the Counterpart Fund would disappear. It is interesting to observe that among the answers the Eos Study gave there was a suggestion of an Asia Marshall Plan to the tune of $150 million to be provided by the United States and also a proposal that restrictions on Japan's trade with mainland China should be eased.

Nothing practical came out of the Eos Study; but its general orientation was favorably received by the authorities and Prime Minister Yoshida approved the establishment of a Commission for Economic Self-Support. The Commission commenced its work in the midst of fighting in Korea. It was still too early to presage the extent of the economic impact of the conflict on Japan. By the time the Economic Self-Support Plan was to be completed, toward the end of 1950, it became increasingly apparent that the windfall dollar income due to "special procurements" promised to be enormous,[8] that the securing of needed imports threatened to be difficult in the face of rapidly rising prices, and that domestic inflation was again a serious problem. The plan was made public in January 1951 and set 1953 as the target date for attaining viability. But one cannot escape the impression that it was a hasty product of transitional character, with one foot still resting on the pre-Korean conflict stage and another foot reaching insecurely toward a new level whose scaffoldings were to be "special procurements" of inordinately large size. In any case, it was much less of a practical plan than an academic exercise in the rearrangement of figures.

Events were moving rapidly. General MacArthur issued a directive to the Japanese government to set up the Police Reserve Corps of 75,000 men in July 1950, rehabilitated *en masse* in October about 10,000 Japanese who were prominent in wartime Japan, purged instead in November 11,300 trade union leaders and others who were suspected of Communist leanings, and completed the 180–degree shift by ordering the investigation of the maximum industrial contribution Japan could make in the circumstances of the gathering storm. For this last purpose, latent industrial capacity was re-estimated. It was tentatively concluded in early 1951 that, on the assumption that plant and

---

[8] It was announced in early December that within five months since the conflict had begun the dollar income of Japan due to "special procurements" had amounted to $170 million, more than the total sum of the proposed Asia Marshall Plan.

equipment were the sole limitational factors, mining and manufacturing production could reach at that time the possible top-level figure of 204 per cent of the 1932–36 average, or 90 per cent more than the actual figure in 1951.[9] Thus this investigation, carried out jointly by the occupation and the Japanese government, was labeled the "Top-Level Study." It was nothing more than an exploration; but when the Japanese delegation went to San Francisco in September 1951 to sign the peace treaty they took with them the so-called "Document B," which was largely based on the Top-Level Study.

Document B did scale down the maximum potential figures indicated in the latter by giving consideration to various other factors whose supply was bound to be limited in the short run. But it had the purpose of impressing upon the United States government Japan's positive intention in the program of United States-Japanese economic cooperation; and the entire program tended to be much more ambitious than warranted.   Of all the plans and projections the Japanese government compiled in the postwar period, Document B was the only one that had target figures of production which actual achievements fell short of. It lacked realism, but at least it bore the by-product of bringing into relief the salient bottlenecks of a program of maximum production; it was in fact its stimulus that led to an ambitious program of electric power development launched in subsequent years.

Planning since Independence, 1952–1959

The coming into effect of the peace treaty in April 1952

[9] See Yujiro Hayashi, *Nihon no Keizai Keikaku (Economic Planning in Japan)* (Tokyo, 1957), pp. 158–61.

provided no special occasion for renewed interest in long-range planning, although Japan was now fully free to be a master of its own economy, as it were, and the task of freeing itself of outside props such as U.S. aid and "special procurements" was nonetheless pressing. Prime Minister Yoshida's dislike for planning prevailed while he was in power.

The "Economic Table for 1957"

There was, however, a practical need for an over-all projection of some sort, inasmuch as the Japanese government wished to obtain developmental loans from the World Bank and the latter had indicated its desire to know in detail the prospective state of the Japanese economy as well as the character of measures the government was prepared to take to regain equilibrium in the normal balance of payments and to guide the flow of investment funds in the most effective, rational manner. To meet this need, the government undertook the preparation of what was then known as the "Economic Table for 1957." As in all the earlier plans and projections, the Economic Stabilization Board was in charge of drafting the Table, except that the ESB was reorganized in July 1952 and renamed the Economic Counsel Board.[10] Therefore the planning officials not only had all the heritage of planning and projection documents but many of them had continued in the same capacity through the vagaries of shifting scenes. Yet, here a new departure was made. Whereas the preceding plans and projections partook of the character, in various adaptations, of a set of accounts balancing materials requirements and supply, the legacy of wartime allocations and control, the Economic

[10] Another reorganization took place in 1955 and the name was changed to the present one, the Economic Planning Agency.

190

Table for 1957 shook off this somewhat clumsy approach and made greater use of growth rate concepts in arriving at the over-all Table for 1957. The year-to-year process was no longer a concern of the planners. Furthermore, the inductive method was de-emphasized. It was candidly stated by an official in charge that their "purpose was much less that of depicting a probable over-all picture without any prejudice as to policy measures than that of giving a plausible garb to the prejudged policy recommendations of (1) electric power development, (2) rapid recovery of the shipbuilding industry, and (3) the special emphasis on agricultural development."[11]

The Okano Scheme

The Table was made public in February 1953 and was rapidly followed in July of the same year by the "Okano Scheme," so named because Mr. Okano was then the minister in charge of the Economic Counsel Board and the government apparently did not wish to commit the entire Cabinet to the Scheme. The Scheme also had a specific purpose in view, namely, to draw out the necessary implications of all-out efforts for the expansion of exports, with an added intent of impressing upon visiting experts from the World Bank, who came in November 1953, Japan's pressing need for external loans to attain economic viability.

The Okano Scheme estimated a shortfall in the current international balance of some $400 million in 1957, the proposed all-out export drive notwithstanding. Robert Garner, Vice-president of the World Bank, who was presented with the Okano Scheme, was apparently disappointed with its half-hearted character and upon his return to the United States made a

[11] Yoshitake Sasaki's statement quoted in *ibid.*, p. 143.

191

critical comment at a meeting of the Foreign Policy Association in New York, saying that:

> So far as I can see, the Japanese government appears to have neither an over-all plan of any sort nor a specific plan of channeling private capital into the most important sectors of the economy. I suggested, therefore, that inasmuch as there was a danger of funds flowing into unimportant sectors the Japanese government might set up an agency which would decide on the priority of investment needs. They objected to this saying that they always preferred a "free enterprise economy" to a "planned economy." I, for one, however, do not see why the government's determination to have private funds flow into the most important channels should conflict with the requirements of a "free enterprise economy."[12]

In retrospect it seems clear that the Okano Scheme was drafted for political rather than economic purposes. Aside from the intent of drawing maximum loans from the World Bank, the Scheme wanted to justify the resuscitation of export cartels. How unrealistic it turned out to be can be seen by contrasting its projection of maximum effort exports for 1957, $1,460 million, with the actual achievement in that year, $2,858 million.

The Scheme for Over-all Development

The last of the plans and projections attempted by the Yoshida Cabinet was the "Scheme for Over-all Development," which was completed in September 1954 in the midst of the gloom of the 1953–54 recession and of the declining volume of "special procurements." In that atmosphere planning officials suddenly awoke to the seriousness of the surplus labor problem

[12] Quoted in *ibid.*, pp. 144–45; here retranslated into English from Japanese.

in Japan. With specific death rates for various age groups having become more or less stabilized at relatively low levels, it was possible in 1954 to estimate the prospective supply of the new labor force in each year up to 1965. If the labor participation ratio was to remain the same as in 1952, Japan faced the task of absorbing each year a net increase in its labor force of approximately one million at least up to 1965. This task was thought to be formidable, especially in view of the fact that the Japanese economy in 1952 admittedly harbored an amount of disguised unemployment variously estimated as the equivalent of five million or more workers.

Experts who worked on the Scheme for Over-all Development apparently felt it would be rather unrealistic to expect to attain the goal of full employment by 1965 under the given constraints; therefore, with some justification, they assumed the gradual decline in the labor participation ratio from 68 per cent of the population between the ages of fourteen and sixty inclusive in 1952 to 62 per cent in 1965. To the prospective labor force in 1965 thus estimated they applied the so-called "Colm Method"[13] to obtain the over-all picture of the Japanese economy in 1965, on the assumption, among others, of about a 3 per cent rise in per hour labor productivity every year. The structure of social accounting and the requirements of growth for specific industries were then estimated in harmony with the target level of real gross national product. The assumptions used in this last step of the projection are too numerous to mention here. In any case, the implication was drawn from the study as to the urgent need of regional development programs which would create new employment opportu-

---

[13] The method used by Gerhard Colm in his study, *The American Economy in 1960* (Washington, D.C.: National Planning Association, 1952).

nities by opening up domestic resources within Japan. Herein lay the real significance of the Scheme for Over-all Development, which also incidentally provided a new methodology for planning which was more fully utilized after the Yoshida Cabinet fell.

The 1956 Five-Year Plan

With the departure of Yoshida, for whom the word "planning" was anathema, the mood among official circles changed markedly. Under the new Hatoyama Cabinet the Economic Counsel Board was renamed the Economic Planning Agency, and the preparation for a study of long-range planning for the Japanese economy was ordered by the Prime Minister. Again the enthusiasm of planning officials, long subdued under the reign of Yoshida, was fired; an extensive, multifaceted study was launched, resulting in the publication in January 1956 of the *Five-Year Plan for Economic Self-Supoprt*.[14] In the sense that no disguise was any longer needed in the use of a word like "planning," it marked a new departure. But the methodology of the planning calculus[15] was essentially the same as in the Scheme for Over-all Development. The basic desiderata were still the twin goals of full employment and economic self-support. The Colm Method, applied earlier, was further refined and was combined with the Harrod-Domar type of growth model to produce framework figures for the target year. The controlling assumption was again a cumulative annual rate of growth in per man productivity of 3 per cent, which had the necessary implication of a 5 per cent annual rate of growth of gross

[14] It encompassed five years from the fiscal year 1956 (April 1, 1956–March 31, 1961).

[15] See, for detail, Shigeto Tsuru, "Empirical Testing of the Macro-Economic Planning in Japan," *Essays on Japanese Economy* (Tokyo, 1958), chap. 6.

national product under the constraint of a 2 per cent rate of growth in the active labor force.

The five-year plan did not stop at simply giving projected framework figures for the target year. It spelled out needed measures to implement the plan both in terms of basic policies and with reference to specific administrative branches of the government. Among the former it is noteworthy that the suppression of a rise in private consumption expenditures in favor of investment in plant and equipment was rather strongly indicated.[16] Otherwise most of the proposed measures were in the nature of wholesale endorsement of the pet ideas of several ministries and probably were utilized by the latter as excuses for demanding increased appropriations in the budget. This was unavoidable inasmuch as the government which drafted the plan took pains to make clear that its basic position was the maximum respect for private initaitive and the minimum resort to any kind of centralized planning, and furthermore because the office of the Economic Planning Agency was the weakest link in the power configuration of the Japanese bureaucracy. As a result, not much came out of the plan in terms of specific measures uniquely associated with its objectives and implications. Need for them was felt less and less as time went on since the Japanese economy, apparently on its own steam, manifested a growth capacity far beyond the expectation of the most sanguine optimists.[17]

---

[16] Such a policy orientation probably stemmed from the assumption of a very high value for the gross capital coefficient or incremental capital-output ratio. Defining it as $V_t/(GNP_{t+1} - GNP_t)$, where "V" stands for gross capital formation including government investment, the "plan" assumed its value to be 5.

[17] The plan targets for fiscal 1960 may be contrasted with the actual achievements to show how wide of the mark the plan turned out to be.

The New Long-Range Economic Plan

Seeing the five-year plan of 1956 becoming rapidly obsolete, the government was obliged to set its sights anew; and the birth of the Kishi Cabinet in 1957 provided a convenient occasion for such a reappraisal. In accordance with a new instruction issued in early August of that year by the Prime Minister, again the machinery of paper-work planners started to function, and it produced rather expeditiously the "New Long-Range Economic Plan," which was approved by the Cabinet in December 1957.

This plan covered the five-year period of fiscal 1958 to fiscal 1962. The basic question which it tried to answer was: What is the optimal rate of growth consistent with the constraints of reasonably full employment and of equilibrium in the international balance of payments? The first of the two constraints would indicate an extremely high rate of growth as a desideratum under the given circumstances; but the second would set a ceiling on the growth rate because of an assumed, somewhat inflexible, behavior of import propensity and the assumed limitation on Japan's export possibilities. A similar problem

	Planned Targets	Actual Achievements
Population (thousands)	93,230	93,407
Active labor force (thousands)	44,860	44,640a)
Real GNP (1955=100)	127.6	162.0
Real per capita consumption (1934–36=100)	135.1	147.5
Index of mining and manufacturing production (1955=100)	167.0	227.3a)
Exportsb) (customs returns in millions of dollars)	$2,720	$4,117a)
Importsc) (millions of dollars)	$2,970	$4,661a)

a) The average or total figure, as the case may be, for the calendar year 1960.
b) The unit value index of Japanese exports rose slightly (8 per cent) between 1955 and 1960.
c) The unit value index of Japanese mports declined by 12.4 per cent between 1955 and 1960.

had presented itself in the drafting of the *Five-Year Plan for Economic Self-Support*. But this time emphasis was clearly laid on stretching the feasible growth rate as far as possible to enable the economy to meet the employment dilemma posed by the twin desiderata; and the 6.5 per cent figure was chosen as the optimal rate. In order to achieve this rate, however, it was realized that the export drive would have to be intensified more than ever and that the lag in capital investment in social overhead would need early correction. Further, one refinement was introduced in the planning calculus, that is, to calculate a set of theoretical base year figures for 1956 by smoothing the fluctuations of the preceding six years. The plan proposed a cumulative rate of growth of 6.5 per cent to be built up on this theoretical base.

Consistency of the plan as a painted picture and its realistic character as a projection may be said to have shown improvement over the earlier plans. But as regards implementation of the plan, that peculiar lack of practical realism which characterized all the earlier plans persisted. The official document states in the opening sentence that: "This plan is to serve as guideposts for economic operation within the basic institutional framework of free enterprise and a free market." And it goes on to specify as "instruments for implementing the plan" "such indirect methods as fiscal, monetary, and trade-and-exchange policies," stating clearly that "the government shall refrain, to the utmost, from resorting to direct control measures."

No doubt these statements revealed the basic orientation of the government. But even within this frame of reference the plan avoided the necessary task of indicating the specific measures needed to reach the plan objectives. For example, the plan implied fiscal outlays of various sorts, and yet no serious effort was made in quantifying the public investment needs except in a few cases, and then in only a perfunctory manner. The statement, "If we are to make a tentative estimate, in an over-all fashion, of the amount of adminitrative investment for agricultural land development corresponding to the growth of farm income at 3.3 per cent per annum, the figure of 230 billion yen might be indicated for the five-year period," certainly does not commit the government to this amount. In fact the ministry in charge was in no way bound by such a "might-be-indicated" figure. It was also most unrealistic to assume that the exchange allocation measure, which was to be continued under the plan, was an "indirect" method.

At any rate, the New Long-Range Economic Plan went the way of most earlier plans and was cast aside as obsolete within two years in the face of a most remarkable growth performance in 1959 and 1960. An unexpectedly favorable turn in the terms of trade made it possible for the Japanese economy to expand faster than the plan had indicated, without immediately incurring the unbearable burden of payments imbalance.

Twice, then, what originally appeared a fairly ambitious plan failed to gauge even approximately the momentum of dynamic growth which seems to be characterizing the Japanese economy today. The stage was set, therefore, at least psychologically, for yet another plan of greater optimism to emerge.

The attractive but somewhat ambiguous slogan "Double Your Income in Ten Years!"[18] was heard in the early months of 1959, especially from the mouth of Mr. Hayato Ikeda, whose

[18] At first it was not made clear whether this meant (1) real income or nominal income, (2) per capita income or national income, or (3) income of a particular person or income corresponding to a specific position or qualification.

ambition to succeed Mr. Kishi as Prime Minister was fast becoming obvious. Apparently for political reasons, Kishi embraced Ikeda's bullish philosophy and gave instructions in November 1959 to work out an income-doubling plan. The Security Pact fracas ousted Kishi from the helm in July 1960 and, as expected, brought Ikeda into the position of premier. The income-doubling mood immediately prevailed in the business world without waiting for any plan of the government; and the latter hastened to complete such a plan, coming out in November 1960 with what is officially known as "The Plan for Doubling National Income." More specifically, the plan calls for the doubling of real gross national product in the ten years between 1961 and 1970, implying an average cumulative annual rate of growth of 7.2 per cent. Of the dozen or more plans and projections the Japanese government has issued in the postwar period, this plan calls for a separate detailed treatment in this study.

The Plan for Doubling National Income

The Character of the Plan

The planning calculus was at once simple and complex— simple because the 7.2 per cent annual rate of growth was the dictate of political decision and could not be altered, complex because the planning officials chose to rationalize this bold target in terms of various economic concepts which had to be harmonized with the prospective reality. For this purpose planners set up a model[19] which purported to show, in the doubled

[19] See Saburo Okita, *Shotoku Baizo Keikaku no Kaisetsu* (*Income-Doubling Plan Explained*) (Tokyo, 1960), pp. 145–55.

gross national product which would be reached in 1970, the nature of the economic activity that would be going on.

The estimates were based on the conditions or relationships expected to prevail because of technical requirements (for example, equipment or materials requirements for production), behavior patterns of the people (consumption habits, for example), or governmental policy decisions. Such conditions or relationships are termed "parameters." Those determined by technical requirements or behavior patterns are "institutional parameters." In the model for the decade ending in 1970 they include such economic quantities as the amount of investment needed per unit of increase in output in various fields (the "capital coefficient"), the increase in imports resulting from each billion yen increase in the gross national product (the "propensity to import"), and the estimated increase in the labor force. Quantities of relationships determined by government policy are policy parameters. Examples are tax rates and the ratio of government investment to gross national product. Some of these were derived in consultation with government ministries. Other policy objectives, such as the improvement of transportation and power facilities and other social overhead capital and the encouragement of an economically rational development of heavy industries, were proposed on the basis of general observation and empirical judgment; and it was assumed that the investment and production in various fields needed to achieve these objectives would be accomplished by 1970. By use of other parameters, other magnitudes were calculated—for example, the volume of total investment, its division between government and private investment, aggregate consumer expenditures, output in various sectors of the economic system, the requirements for raw materials, the level of imports, employment in various sectors, consumer income, and government income and expenditures. The set of magnitudes thus obtained was called "the framework." The calculated increase in the demand for labor and for various types of materials and products did not always coincide at first with the calculated increase in the supply. Adjustments were then made to achieve consistency, which was the major aim of the first step. Some of these adjustments were in policy parameters; it was assumed that the government would adjust its policies to achieve a smooth working of the economic system. Trial and error was the method employed in arriving at a final consistent set of values for all the variables involved.

In this process various magnitudes and relationships not determined in advance of the calculations were decided in a passive manner as a result of them. An example is the growth in per man productivity. With the assumed increase of 7.2 per cent per year in gross national product and the estimated increase in the labor force, the increase in output per man was automatically determined. It came out at 5.6, 5.5, and 5.5 per cent per year in the primary, secondary, and tertiary industries respectively. The rates seem too uniform, considering the different characters of these industries, but by the nature of the model this situation could not be avoided. Furthermore, in the course of successive approximations it was often found that the original estimate of institutional parameters resulted in implying a relation which on reflection appeared somewhat unrealistic. In such cases even the value of the institutional parameters was retouched. A case in point is the propensity to consume, which, if unrevised, would indicate a ratio of individual saving out of disposable income rising beyond 20 per cent in the later years of the plan. In this case, therefore, the ratio was arbitrarily revised downward. In other words, the planning calculus involved compromise of all sorts throughout. This process of compromise, however, was never permitted to cast doubt on the feasibility of doubling real gross national product in ten years.

Imperfect as the planning calculus may have been, building the model itself was not very important in this instance. The nature of the plan was admittedly political. Furthermore, the basic premise of the income-doubling plan was that the private business sector had its own dynamism to grow fast and that it remained for the government adequately to provide complementary facilities of all kinds which were properly its responsibility. Aside from the question of whether or not the prognosis of dynamism of the private business world was correct, one may say that the plan was marked by realism for the first time, in the sense that it clearly demarcated the sphere of government's direct responsibility and attempted to spell out needed measures within that limited sphere. In contrast to earlier plans and projections, whose proposals bore little relationship to the measures actually executed from year to year, the degree of realism now introduced was an innovation.

Policy Obijectives of the Plan and Planning Procedures

Probing of what needed to be done and what the government, committed to the basic tenet of free enterprise, was able to do was marked with pragmatic realism and resulted in setting up the following five major policy objectives, or "pillars" as they were called, of the income-doubling plan.

1. *Strengthening of social overhead capital.* It has been statistically established that social overhead capital in a broad sense of the

term has lagged woefully behind the most remarkable boom in private investment in the past decade. In particular, roads and highways, port facilities, the supply of industrial water, and the strategic land space for industrial development have proven to be bottlenecks for further economic growth. And of course these belong to the sphere of work for which the government is peculiarly fitted to assume direct responsibility.

2. *Favoring of a shift in industrial structure toward heavy industries.* It is generally observed that the progress of an economy toward an advanced stage is marked by an ever-increasing relative weight of heavy industries such as engineering and chemical. Not only is the value-added productivity high in these fields but also the structure of consumer demand becomes slanted more and more toward consumer durables as per capita income rises. This is basically a natural development which will take place even without any government encouragement. But the plan proposes measures of expediting this process as an integral part of doubling real gross national product in ten years.

3. *Promotion of trade and international economic cooperation.* It is recognized that the ability to pay for needed imports is going to be an ever-present bottleneck for the rapid growth of the Japanese economy inasmuch as that economy depends upon imports for the major part of its industrial raw materials. If equilibrium in the international balance of payments is to be maintained while output grows at the rate indicated in the plan, exports will have to grow at the annual rate of 10 per cent, which implies the increasing of Japan's share in world trade in the coming decade. This will be possible only if the manufacturing industry of Japan keeps up its high rate of growth in productivity while trade is further liberalized. Promotion of international economic cooperation is suggested in this connection, for the rapid growth of developing countries, stimulated by outside aid, is expected to redound to the aiding nation's favor through the rising volume of imports by the developing countries from the technically more advanced ones.

4. *Raising the quality of human resources and the promotion of science and technology.* In the era of the so-called scientific-industrial

203

revolution it is becoming more and more obvious that investment in scientific research and technical education is a vital part of investment for economic growth.   The thinking of government officials in Japan has not been sufficiently oriented in the past toward the close connection between science and technology, and economics.   It is proposed that this failing now be mended through a joint effort of the government and the private sector.

5.   *Mitigation of "dual structure" gaps and securing of social stability.* In spite of the remarkable growth the Japanese economy attained in the past decade, it has to be conceded that the traditionally prevalent "dual structure" in the economy was hard to erase. "Dual structure" refers to the coexistence of a technically lagging low-wage sector of small enterprises and small productive plants with a modern high-wage sector of large enterprises and plants, and the lack of labor mobility between the two sectors.   Aside from the problem of social tension which ensues as a result of continuing, or even increasing, gaps, it is inevitable that the task of improving labor mobility will become one of the urgent items on the agenda in the coming decade as the rate of increase in the labor force will begin to dwindle after the middle 1960's because of the earlier decline in the birth rate.   If the "dual structure" gaps are not mitigated automatically through rapid growth of the economy, it is up to the government to do something about them.

Of these five policy objectives it seems that the greatest emphasis was laid on the first, that is, "strengthening of social overhead capital."   Thus a question may be posed here as to what criteria were employed in the planning procedures in order to arrive at the final figures of the total amount and components of social overhead investment in the projected plan.

For the purpose of the plan the government's contribution to the maintenance and expansion of social overhead capital was defined as "administrative investment" and specifically included the following three subcategories: investment to strengthen the basic structure of the economy (road construction, port facilities, agricultural and forestry development, and industrial water); investment for public welfare (residential construction, public welfare facilities, and environmental health facilities); and investment for conservation of resources (reforestation, water control, and rehabilitation after natural disasters).

The first step in the planning procedure was to estimate statistically the actual proportion of such "administrative investment" to the total gross national product in the past. This was found to have ranged from 4 to 6 per cent in the postwar years. Private capital formation in plant and equipment was generally about three times as great. Empirical observation suggested that the facilities provided by "administrative investment" were beginning to be severely overtaxed; their capacity was beginning to be markedly inadequate to meet the demands on them. Thus it was arbitrarily decided in the first instance that the ratio to gross national product should be raised to 7 per cent during the plan years, aiming to reach the level of one half of private fixed capital formation. But when the total sum thus calculated was broken down into various subcategories, the result could not satisfy all the sponsoring ministries. The final compromise was struck by raising the ratio to gross national product to 7.9 per cent. Therefore disposable individual income suffered a slight reduction in the plan from the magnitude initially calculated.

What criteria to use in breaking down the total into various subcategories presented a major theoretical problem. Planning officials wanted to avoid "pork barrel" distribution and yet could not agree upon any objective criteria which could meet the test of economic rationality. Since some kind of rule of thumb was needed, it was proposed to apply what was called "the weighted elasticity criteria."[20]   By this method the total projected amount of "administrative investment" was distributed among the three subcategories mentioned above.   The subcategory figures thus estimated were further broken down into final categories such as road building and port facilities on the basis of practical consideration and empirical judgments.

[20] The method involved calculating the average elasticity over 1956 to 1960 of each subcategory of "administrative investment" with respect to the weighted average of three indexes, that is, mining and manufacturing production, population, and per capita income.   (By elasticity is meant the ratio of the percentage increase of the category of "administrative investment" to the weighted average percentage increase in the three indexes.) Different weights were used for each subcategory as follows:

	Basic Structure Investment	Public Welfare Investment	Conservation Investment
Mining and manufacturing production	6	1	4
Population	2	3	3
Per capita income	2	6	3

The rationale here was that the basic structure investment, for example, would have to be expanded more in response to the rise in mining and manufacturing production than in response to the rise in per capita income, whereas public welfare investment would be the reverse.   Annual changes in the three indexes were averaged for each year with appropriate weights for each subcategory.   Thus, whereas the rate of change from 1955 to 1956 was:

+22.4% for mining and manufacturing production

+1.1% for population

+7.4% for per capita income,

the combined index would show:

+15.1% for basic structure investment

+ 6.9% for public welfare investment

+11.5% for conservation investment.

On the other hand, the annual rate of change of each subcategory of "administrative investment" was calculated, and it was divided by the contemporary rate of change of the corresponding combined index to obtain a measure of elasticity.   Thus again, for example, since the basic structure investment rose by 18 per cent between 1955 and 1956, its elasticity for that period was found to be 18.0/15.1, which equaled 1.192.   For each of the subcategories of "administrative investment," the calculated elasticities were averaged over the five years 1956–1960, and then such averages were applied to the projected rates of change of the three indexes mentioned earlier, again combining the latter with appropriate weights for each subcategory.   In

There is little doubt that the authors of the plan would readily concede that the planning procedure explained in the preceding footnote was not based on any principle of economic rationality. A semblance of rationality was given by the use of "appropriate" weights separately designed for each subcategory; but the procedure was essentially that of an extrapolation of the past trend. Such as they were, the "weighted elasticity criteria" did serve a purpose by giving apparently neutral guideposts to different lines of activities which competed for the limited governmental funds. Undoubtedly practical compromise was made easier through this procedure.

Planning procedures for the other policy objectives were also more or less the same. For example, as a part of the program for "raising the quality of human resources and the promotion of science and technology," investment in research was to be expanded. The ratio of such investment to national income was calculated to have been 0.9 per cent in 1958. The similar ratio in the United States has been estimated to be around 2 per cent in recent years. The question was how fast Japan should approach the relative level the United States had attained. No theory could come to the aid of the planners in this regard; the final decision was again based on practical considerations, and the figure of 1.3 per cent was chosen for the target year of 1970. On the whole one cannot avoid the impression that

the case of basic structure investment the average elasticity turned out to be 1.642. Projected annual rates of change for the plan period were:

+10.4% for mining and manufacturing production
+ 0.9% for population
+ 6.6% for per capita income.

Their weighted average appropriate to the basic structure investment would be 7.74 per cent. Multiplying this figure by 1.642. we obtain the value of 12.7 per cent as the appropriate annual rate of change for the basic structure investment for the plan period.

although the policy objectives were not only laudable but also highly practical, the procedure used in quantifying mutually competing projects was little more than a matter of compromise, occasionally appealing to esoteric calculations to set up a defense line for the planners against the overzealous demands of sponsoring ministries.

So far as those policy objectives which depend largely on the initiative of the private sector were concerned, the plan confined itself either to proclaiming generalities or to indicating desirable directions of change without specifying how to accomplish them. A case in point is the second policy objective, the "favoring of a shift in industrial structure toward heavy industries." What the plan does in this connection is first to give a detailed prospectus of a desirable pattern of the individual structure for 1970 and then to spell out measures needed to attain it, as follows:

1. Modernization of capital equipment, the full utilization of economies of scale, the further standardization of commodity specifications, and so on.
2. Accumulation of internal savings by firms.
3. Securing cheap energy sources and raw materials from abroad.
4. Improvement in the locational environment for industries.
5. Encouragement of technological research and training of engineers.
6. Modernization of small-size firms.

Few would question the desirability of these measures but everyone would ask what concrete and specific steps the government proposed to undertake in these regards. The plan document, after enumerating the above measures, simply appends a short sentence, saying that, "In order to attain these objectives it will be necessary that the government does its best in performing its supporting and expediting functions."[21] The sentence leaves the most important question of specific procedures unanswered. But it is quite possible that the omission was deliberate so that the ministries concerned could work out concrete proposals for needed legislation and other administrative measures as the occasion might demand.

Implementation of the Plan

Theoretically speaking, implementation of the policy objectives set forth was certainly within the capabilities of the government. In fact, a stranger who studies the Japanese scene from outside might suppose that the Economic Planning Agency, possibly under the strong leadership of the Prime Minister, could serve as a coordinating administrative body looking after the progress of the plan's implementation, so far as these policy objectives are concerned, with a power to suggest needed measures and appropriations as the occasion demands. Theoretically such a supposition is warranted because Japan's administrative structure as it exists today permits this to happen if the Prime Minister decides to exercise his leadership in this direction.

But the fact of the matter is otherwise. So long as an over-all plan drafted by the Economic Planning Agency lacked realism in the sense that it remained largely an intellectual exercise, it could be regarded by other ministries as a matter requiring simply ceremonial approval. But once a plan acquires a measure of realism, as in the case of the 1960 plan, the ministries

[21] Later in the document the implication of such phrases as "accumulation of internal savings by firms" and "modernization of small-scale firms" is further developed. But again what is found is an all-around enumeration of possible measures in support of these desiderata; nowhere does the document permit itself to be pinned down on what the government specifically proposes to do.

concerned, such as Finance, Agriculture and Forestry, International Trade and Industry, and Construction, awake suddenly to the need of guarding their vested interests and attempt to take advantage of the plan for extending their own interests without in any way surrendering ministerial prerogative. The weakness of the Economic Planning Agency in the power configuration of the Japanese bureaucracy then becomes more apparent than ever. In practically no administrative matters can the Economic Planning Agency exercise an independent initiative or power of coordination. It is like an assembly plant which has to make a façade of coordinated harmony out of parts supplied by others beyond its control.

Nevertheless there does remain a task for the Economic Planning Agency, namely, to follow the actual progress of the economy to check discrepancies of the plan from reality; but even here the Agency is not empowered in any way to initiate measures for correcting them. The only thing it can do is to sponsor periodically, twice a year or so, the meeting of the Policy Coordination Subcommittee of the Economic Council, a consultative body (composed of professors, bankers, and businessmen) attached to the Agency, and to have the Subcommittee chairman make public observations of a rather general sort. Needless to say, such observations are not binding on any executive branch of the government.

Theoretically speaking, there does exist in Japan today a powerful lever through which both the direction and the magnitude of investment activities can be influenced by the government—that is, a string of government financing institutions, most of which have come into existence in the postwar period, through which a sizable part of investment resources are channeled into various sectors of the economy.

The over-all category which subsumes all the new governmental financing is "treasury loans and investments"; and its total projected amount for the fiscal year 1962 was 859.6 billion yen, or more than one third of the current account budget figure of the central government. Until 1955 "treasury loans and investments" played a very important role as a source of fixed investment funds in the private sector, accounting for as much as 30 per cent or more of the total. They were largely concentrated in the strategic industries of steel, coal, electricity, and shipping. Subsequently, their relative weight, at least in the quantitative sense, has declined, first to 17 per cent in 1956 and then gradually to 9 per cent in 1961. Emphasis has shifted to those sectors which found it difficult to obtain funds through internal financing, namely, small-scale industries, agriculture and fisheries, and social overhead structures.

Government financing institutions are of two kinds: "loan special accounts," which depend for sources of funds upon postal savings, post-office life insurance, and postal annuity premiums; and special banks and finance corporations of which the Japan Development Bank is the biggest. "Loan special accounts" are operated largely through the Trust Fund Beruau of the Ministry of Finance; and it is important to note the fact that the relative weight of people's savings funds flowing into this channel has been traditionally of a substantial order of magnitude. In fact the postal saving system is the biggest "bank" in Japan, with 16,000 branches all over the country. With its tremendous financing power, however, the Trust Fund Bureau does not possess much maneuverability because it is severely restricted by law in its lending activities. As of the end of August 1962, for example, more than 80 per cent of its assets were composed of central and local government securities and loans to governmental institutions. The remainder was accounted for by bank debentures and corporate bonds of semi-governmental corporations.

As for special banks and finance corporations, eleven of them are in active existence in 1963, all having been established in the postwar years with the government subscribing the entire capital. The list which follows is in the order of establishment, with the capitalization in parentheses.

1949   People's Finance Corporation (¥ 20 billion)
1950   Housing Loan Corporation (¥ 72 billion)
1951   Export-Import Bank of Japan (¥ 98.3 billion)
        Japan Development Bank (¥ 233.9 billion)
1953   Agriculture, Forestry and Fisheries Finance Corporation
        (¥ 109.3 billion)
        Small-Business Finance Corporation (¥ 24.1 billion)
1956   Hokkaido and Tohoku Development Finance Corporation
        (¥ 2.5 billion)
1957   Local Public Enterprise Finance Corporation (¥ 2.4
        billion)
1958   Small-Business Credit Insurance Corporation (¥ 18.3
        billion)
1960   Medical Care Facilities Finance Corporation (¥ 5.5
        billion)
1961   Fund for External Economic Cooperation (¥ 10.4 billion)

The names of these institutions are sufficiently specific to suggest their respective tasks except, perhaps, the People's Finance Corporation and the Japan Development Bank. The former is "for the purpose of supplying business funds to those individuals who generally find it difficult to obtain them from ordinary banks and financial institutions." In other words, it is a special bank for short-term loans favoring small business

212

enterprises, while the Small-Business Finance Corporation is engaged in longer term loan activities. The Japan Development Bank, on the other hand, was established as successor to the Reconstruction Finance Corporation and was given the task of "supplementing and promoting the lending operations of ordinary financial institutions, through long-term lending, toward reconstruction of the economy and development of industries." Beside the original capital, subscribed wholly by the government, the Bank has borrowed money from time to time from the Trust Fund Bureau and other government sources and by the end of August 1962 had loans outstanding almost three times its original capitalization. One gets the impression that of all the government financing institutions this is the one that could effectively be utilized for planning purposes with sufficient impact and flexibility. In actual fact, however, the Bank laid special emphasis on electricity and shipping in its early years of operation; and even at the end of August 1962 almost 80 per cent of its loans outstanding was more or less frozen in these two fields. There is a tendency in Japan that once an institution is established it becomes committed to the promotion of a set of specific interests and cannot easily be bent to meet the needs of over-all planning.

In summary it may be said that the Plan for Doubling National Income (1) is not a *plan* for doubling national income but limits itself to setting out certain policy objectives, within the capabilities of the central government, on the assumption that the private sector has its own dynamism for doubling income in ten years; and (2) *appears* to be a coordinated plan so far as the public sector is concerned but in fact is being administered largely by the various ministries as if no over-all plan existed.

Thus the practical consequence of the plan was, firstly, to give

213

several ministries occasion for advancing their pet projects to have them legitimatized under the name of the plan, leaving the mode of implementation unchanged as before; and, secondly, to create a general mood in the private sector that the government would underwrite any capacity expansion which aims at meeting the increased demand projected in the plan. This latter consequence has proved to be especially important as the plan years progressed. When the annual growth rate of 7.2 per cent is projected for the coming decade under the name of a governmental plan, it is perfectly natural for each private enterprise to strive to capture the maximum share of the marginal increase in the market and compete with the others in expanding its capacity as fast as it can. An industry is typically composed of several or more firms; and the inevitable consequence has been that the total capacity expansion in several basic industries has turned out to be greater than warranted. The signal of overexpansion was not immediately forthcoming, for by the nature of the case investment supports investment and the general overexpansion justifies, at least for a short period, the overexpansion of basic industries.

What transpired in 1961, the first year of the plan, was typically a situation of this kind. The total amount of private capital formation in plant and equipment in 1961 is estimated to have topped the amount projected for 1970—the amount calculated to correspond to twice the gross national product of 1960. Some kind of administrative warning was in order. A warning did come in June 1961 from the Subcommittee chairman of the Economic Council, but the Prime Minister kept on maintaining his optimistic composure and the business world apparently felt no reason for an investment cutback.

The announcement in the fall of 1961 that Japan would

liberalize her trade to the extent of 90 per cent by the fall of 1962 gave further impetus to what was called "modernization investment." The investment boom went on unabated. By the end of 1961 normal indications of an excessive investment boom clearly showed themselves. Thus imports started running far ahead of exports; the gap between loans and deposits in commercial banks widened further; and central bank credit, which had maintained the level of about 40 per cent of the bank notes outstanding from 1958 through 1960, began rising rapidly in 1961 and finally passed the 100 per cent mark in February 1962. Meanwhile analysis of the financial statements of manufacturing corporations compiled by the Bank of Japan revealed a contrasting picture as to the movement of capital-cost elements between the previous boom of 1955–56 and that of 1960–61, as shown in Table 2:

TABLE 2

RATIOS OF CAPITAL COSTS TO VALUE ADDED IN MANUFACTURING[a]

(Per cent)

	Depreciation	Interest Charges	Total Capital Cost[b]
1955: Second half	14.5	13.1	27.5
1956: First half	14.5	11.2	25.7
1956: Second half	13.6	10.2	23.8
1960: First half	16.1	13.3	29.5
1960: Second half	16.5	13.6	30.0
1961: First half	18.3	13.8	32.0
1961: Second half	18.2	14.9	33.1

a) Compiled from Bank of Japan, *Analysis of Financial Statements of Industrial Corporations* (semiannual publication, in Japanese).

b) Decimal figures may not agree because of rounding.

"Value added" in an industry is the value of the goods produced minus the cost of the materials and other goods and services purchased from other industries in the process. Thus value added in automobile manufacturing is the value of the automobiles produced minus the cost to the automobile industry of the raw materials, components, power, and so on which it buys from other industries. Value added is composed of wages and salaries, depreciation allowances and interest, rents and profits.[22] Whereas the 1955–56 boom was accompanied by a steady decline in the ratio of capital costs to total value added in manufacturing as a whole, the 1960–61 boom tells an entirely opposite story. In the first half of 1961 capital costs were the highest percentage of total value added recorded in any postwar period. The explanation seems to be that in the boom of 1955–56 the degree of utilization of plant capacity increased, as it usually does in a cyclical upswing. The increase in production without an appreciable increase in the capital equipment used tends to lower the ratio of capital costs to value added. On the other hand, the 1960–61 boom was accompanied by so great an increase in capacity that in spite of the increase in production the degree of plant utilization did not increase, and a rise in the ratio of capital costs to labor costs occurred. Furthermore, the "income-doubling mood" stimulated the general rise in wages; and wherever the rise could not be absorbed by increased productivity, as in service industries, printing and publishing, public utilities, and education, prices rose. Thus the consumer price index of December 1961 registered a rise of 10.2 per cent above the average for 1960.

The essential character of the Plan for Doubling National Income as a plan in the politico-economic setting of present-day Japan is well revealed in these indications. Were it not for the political commitment of the Prime Minister to the plan, these indications, most of which were patent already in the

[22] Taxes paid by business firms sometimes are also included.

216

fall of 1961, would have brought about some administrative measures of moderation sooner. But it seems that a lesson will be learned in the manner of a child who ignores his mother's warning and burns his finger. The lesson is that optimism of the government *can* be highly contagious, but real planning requires more than slogan making, in fact, more than paper work no matter how realistic it may be.

Chapter 12

THE ECONOMIC PROBLEMS OF JAPAN
——PRESENT AND FUTURE——

[1964]

This essay was originally given in a lecture form as a Dyason Memorial Lecture in Australia in 1964 and was subsequently written out and published in the *Australian Outlook*, December 1964. In a sense, this may be read as a sequel to Chapter 10 although the latter was intended for academic audience and this one for much wider public.

I

I SHOULD LIKE TO BEGIN with two quotations both of which, we may say, reflected the common sense of experts at the time they were written. One is by the late Lord Keynes writing in *The Eugenics Review* in 1937:

Past experience shows that a greater cumulative increment than one percent per annum in the standard of life has seldom proved practicable. Even if the fertility of invention would permit more, we can not easily adjust ourselves to a greater rate of change than this involves. There may have been one or two decades in this

country [U.K.] during the past hundred years when improvement
has proceeded at the rate of one percent per annum.   But generally
speaking the rate of improvement seems to have been somewhat
less than one percent per annum cumulative.[1]

Keynes sounds conservative here; but he was not far wrong.
Researches on long-range economic growth of a nation, which
became especially active after the war in a number of countries,
reveal that, for example in the United States, the average rate
of growth of real net product per capita per decade was 9.7
percent over the almost eighty-year period of 1869 to 1948,[2]
which means that per annum cumulative growth rate was
clearly less than one percent.   The best showing in this study
as a percentage growth per decade was registered in the comparison of two overlapping decades: 1869–78 and 1874–83, i.e.,
the decade rate of 30.1 percent, or about 2.7 percent per annum
cumulative.   Studies on most of the European countries have
come out with a similar result,[3] and the judgement of Lord
Keynes appears to be well justified.

The second quotation is from Dr E.A. Ackerman, a natural
resources specialist who served with General MacArthur's
staff at the time of occupation in Japan, writing in 1948
after having made exhaustive studies on Japan's potential
resources.

In the light of an analysis of its resources, the Japan of the next
three decades appears likely to have one of two aspects if its population continues to grow to 100 million or more.   (1) It may have

[1] *The Eugenics Review*, April 1937, p. 16.
[2] S. Kuznets and R. Goldsmith, *Income & Wealth of the United States, Trends and Structures*, 1952, p. 55.
[3] See, in particular, United Nations, *Growth and Stagnation in the European Economy*, 1954, p. 233.

a standard of living equivalent to that of 1930–34 if foreign financial assistance is continued indefinitely. (2) It may be 'self-supporting', but with internal political, economic and social distress and a standard of living gradually approaching the bare subsistence level. Either of these alternatives seems more likely than that of a Japan which will have made itself self-supporting at a 1930–34 standard through foreign trade and improved resources utilization.[4]

The reason that the 1930–34 standard is mentioned here is that the Far Eastern Commission, which was the policy-making body of allied powers on occupied Japan, had announced in January 1947 that it 'determines as a matter of policy that the peaceful needs of the Japanese people should be defined as being substantially the standard of living prevailing in Japan during the period of 1930–34'. It is estimated that the per capita level of real consumption around 1947–48 was about forty percent below this prescribed level. The pessimism of Dr Ackerman was shared widely among the Japanese themselves, especially because the reparation settlement was then still pending and the worst could yet be expected.

The two quotations, one from Lord Keynes and the other from Dr Ackerman, as I said, reflected the common sense judgements of experts at the time each one of them was written. With hindsight, however, we now say that they were utterly wrong. Lord Keynes' reflection, which was meant to apply to most of the advanced countries today, would now be regarded as completely defeatist by leaders as well as by the people of western nations—would in fact be considered preposterously low by Prime Minister Ikeda of Japan. Dr Ackerman's prediction, on the other hand, has already proved definitely wrong. In

[4] E.A. Ackerman, *Japanese Natural Resources*, 1949, p. 528.

terms of per capita real income—or any other per capita measure such as real consumer spending or real GNP—Japan succeeded in recovering to the 1930–34 level within five or six years after the statement was made by Dr Ackerman, attaining at the same time the status of 'self-supporting' economy without any 'internal political, economic and social distress' to speak of. At present, the per capita standard of living of Japan is about twice that of the 1930–34 level, slightly higher or lower depending upon the different measures for the standard we take.

In view of this, we may legitimately ask how and why is it that considered judgements of first-rate specialists in the field only a decade or two decades earlier turned out to be so wrong. Economists, in particular, are obligated to answer this question; and I am going to make a try at this in so far as the matter concerns Japan.

II

Before attempting my own explanation, however, of what appears to be an exceptional experience of the postwar Japan, I think it is fair for me to assume that most of you will be interested in some relevant figures in order that you will be able to visualize in your own mind the general order of magnitude involved.

In order not to bother you with too many figures, I am going to make use of GNP alone. This, as you may know, summarizes a nation's total economic activities into one figure in such a way that whatever total you obtain can be considered as the sum of personal consumption expenditures, gross domestic private capital formation including replacement, government purchases of goods and services, and the surplus on external accounts. In the first instance, the figures are obtained in terms of current prices. But since the price level changes, often substantially, from year to year, the comparison of current price figures is frequently misleading. Therefore, in order to obtain the so-called 'real' figures, we go through the process of what is called 'deflating', i.e., the process of eliminating from the current price figures of GNP the influence of price changes. Thus we obtain a series of real GNP figures for Japan from 1946, that is the first full postwar year, to 1964, the current year. The current year figure, of course, is still a somewhat uncertain estimate.

Economic growth in the real world is never smooth. Weather conditions may affect agricultural crops accidentally; and again the export market for certain products could often be volatile. Therefore, in order to minimize the accidental character of the year we may choose for points of comparison, let us take the average of three years at three different points of time in the above time span of 1946 to 1964: the average of 1946, '47 and '48 as the immediate postwar period, the average of 1953, '54 and '55 as marking the intermediate point, and the average of 1962, '63 and '64 as the latest period. Now, if we take the immediate postwar figure and assume it to be 100, the average for the intermediate point comes out to be 188, which means that the annual rate of growth was 9.4 percent. Then next, if we take this intermediate point figure and assume it to be 100, the average for the latest three years comes out to be 229, which means that the annual rate of growth was 9.6 percent. In other words, for almost two decades the Japanese economy can be said to have maintained consistently an annual rate of growth higher than nine percent. If you wish to obtain the growth rate on a per capita basis, all you have to do is to subtract from the figures I have just mentioned the average annual rate of growth of population, which was approximately 1.5 percent, much higher in the early postwar years because of the repatriation and the 'baby-boom' and lower (one percent or less) in the period after 1954. We may conclude, therefore, that through the postwar period as a whole up to now the per capita real GNP in Japan grew on the average at the rate of about eight percent, a little more slowly in the first half and a little more rapidly in the latest half.

No one, standing in the midst of the debris wrought by wartime destruction as Japan surrendered in August 1945, dreamed, even in one's wildest dreams, of the possibility of Japan's attaining such a remarkable record of recovery and progress beyond. We again ask the question: how was this possible? what was the secret of this miraculous success?

III

Let me hasten to say that in general there is no miracle in one's regaining one's normal weight after prostration through sickness, provided proper care is taken in the process of recovery. Suppose, for example, I suffered an attack of consumption and my weight before that was 150 pounds. During the sickness my weight, let us assume, hit the bottom of 125 pounds; but after a while I became cured of the disease and started to gain weight again, regaining my old weight of 150 pounds, let us say, in one year. This is a 'rate of growth' per annum of 20 percent. No one would call such a regaining of weight miraculous unless the recovery from the sickness itself was miraculous for some other reason.

Similarly, it certainly cannot be denied that there was an

element of 'regaining one's own normal weight,' as it were, in the process of post-war growth in Japan. If this is the case, there arises immediately a question: when can we say did the special period of post-defeat rehabilitation end in the case of Japan? Was it one year after the surrender? Or was it ten years after? Or, we may even ask, are we still in that rehabilitation stage?

An answer to such a question is not easy to give. If it were possible, as in the case of a convalescent person regaining his normal weight, to identify a certain level of production or per capita income as 'normal' for that country, it would be a simple enough matter to put our finger on a particular year and say that that country ended the rehabilitation stage in that year. This, however, cannot be done. An economy in the modern world is, in one sense or another, always on the move. And first of all, it is not easy to pick out any particular year in the prewar period and say that was the 'normal' year for that country. One has a number of choices here, for example, in the case of Japan. Should we take the average of 1930 to '34 as the Far Eastern Commission did? Or the average of 1934 to '36 as has become conventional lately? Or the year 1938 as is usually done for European countries? Depending on which one of these standards we adopt, we come out with a different answer as to the terminal year to rehabilitation; and there can be no *a priori* ground to prefer one to the other. I am not saying, however, that it is meaningless to do this kind of comparison. Provided that one is aware of the limitations of this procedure, there is no denying the fact that one can gain useful information on the rough state of affairs by arbitrarily choosing a particular year as 'the prewar normal' and trying to find out when that level was regained in the postwar period. If, for example, the average of 1934–36 is taken as 'the prewar normal' for Japan, the year in which per capita real income regained that level was 1953, and if either 1938 or '39 is chosen as 'the prewar normal', the terminal year of rehabilitation comes out to be 1957.

There is, however, a more sophisticated criterion for this problem.   It is to assume that an economy in the modern world is inherently a growing economy.   The tempo of growth may be suspended for a while or even reversed in the negative direction by accidents, earthquake, wars and what have you. But sooner or later it will bounce back, not to some kind of a static normal, but to the appropriate position on the constantly rising trend line.   The upward slope of this trend line could differ from country to country; but one can safely assume a given slope for a particular country for a stretch of, let us say, a few decades at least.   Now, Japan did have such an upward sloping trend line before the war of approximately 2.5 percent rate of growth per annum for the real per capita GNP.   Suppose you extend it beyond 1941 to the future and compare this hypothetical line of potentialities with the actual record, which, needless to say, suffered a precipitous decline through the war and started to rise again sharply after the war.   The relevant question under this assumption is: when did the actual line intersect from below the hypothetical line?   The year when this occurred would be the year when the Japanese economy caught up with its own potentialities.   And there can be little surprise if in the process of catching up with oneself the economy appeared to manifest an exceptionally rapid rate of growth. Such is the reasoning of the sophisticated version; and if you prefer to subscribe to this, the terminal year of rehabilitation falls as recently as 1962.

But, after all, economics is much more than these statistics and trend lines. Even when we have no knowledge of statistical rehabilitation, we are aware, by the feel of our skin, so to speak, of the abnormalities attendant to the exceptional period; and more often than not our intuitive reaction as *dramatis personae* on the practical stage of economic activities is an honest reflection of what is normal and what is not. For example, when German citizens in the post-first World War period experienced daily that astronomical inflation of their currency, they knew, irrespective of what statisticians might have told them, that rehabilitation would not have occurred until that inflation was over. The same was the case with the Japanese this time, although the viciousness of the price spiral was not as horrendous as a generation earlier in Germany. Then too, so long as there existed the over-riding influence of noneconomic policy decisions by the occupation authorities on the economic life of the country, whether paternalistic or otherwise, one could not conduct one's economic calculations on the individualistic basis which would normally be the case under capitalism Japan was. There was artificial restrictions on trade on the one hand and unilateral aid from the United States on the other. There were purges of economic personnel often based on political grounds. Far-reaching reforms were instituted on the initiative of the occupation authorities, often without sufficient regard to the contemporary requirements of the economy.

All these things and others were, of course, taken by the Japanese as inevitable—but inevitable only for a time: in other words, as inevitable abnormalities which would sooner or later disappear from the scene. In fact, they did disappear fairly soon one by one. The postwar inflation of substantial magnitude ended, for all practical purposes, by the spring of 1949,

226

when the single exchange standard was set up at the rate which still prevails today. The impact of occupation policies on the economy, on the other hand, can be said to have lasted, in a general sense, until the Peace Treaty became effective in April 1952. But since the occupation authorities themselves, by the end of 1948, started taking the initiative in restoring in Japan the efficacy of the price mechanism and the system of free enterprise in general, the abnormality referred to, which may have lingered on beyond 1949, was not of a disruptive character in the latter years. Even the abrupt termination of the special type of U.S. aid to its occupied areas (the so-called GARRIOA aid) in June 1951 did not have any disruptive effect on the Japanese economy, since the 'special procurements' by the United Nations for the Korean compaign smoothed the transition.

Looking at these, which we may call 'qualitative' aspects of postwar abnormalities, it is my feeling—and I cannot say that it is more than a feeling—that most of them either disappeared or could be taken in stride by 1953, that is, one year after political independence was achieved. If such a judgement is justified, then, along with the consideration that Japan's per capita real income regained the prewar average of 1934–36 also in 1953, we may mark that year or thereabouts as the terminal date for the postwar rehabilitation and abnormalities. And if this judgement holds true, it is still incumbent on us to answer the question why it is that the decade subsequent to that year witnessed a most remarkable annual growth rate of more than eight percent for per capita real GNP. Compare this with Lord Keynes' reflection in 1937 that 'a greater cumulative increment than one percent per annum in the standard of life has seldom proved practicable'; and we become aware that we really face here a formidable task of economic explanation.

IV

An attempt at full explanation of this problem would require weighing of all kinds of factors with appropriate empirical evidence, and had better be done on an academic rostrum. What I intend to do here is to single out, at the risk of appearing to commit oversimplification, what I consider to be the most important element in the situation, and then to enumerate a few supporting factors which were characteristic of Japan.

In preparing the ground for my major point, let me digress a little into the realm of elementary economic theory which may be quite obvious to most of you. Suppose you are managing a firm manufacturing a certain product—let us say, for simplicity, the product is cement. Suppose, further, that your firm developed a certain technological innovation which enables you to reduce the cost of manufacturing cement, say, by ten percent. You now have a choice among three alternatives and/or any combination of them: (1) you could lower the selling price of cement; or (2) you could simply garner the extra margin of revenue over cost as your profit without changing the price of cement; or (3) you could distribute that extra margin to your employees in the form of wage increase. As a matter of fact, some kind of a combination of these three things takes place in the real world. If competition is keen in the cement industry, either for the reason that there are a large number of makers in the field, some of whom may adopt a similar cost-reducing innovation, or for the reason that there exists a product which can serve as a cheap substitute for cement, you probably will not be able to avoid lowering the price of your product to some extent. Again, if you are confronted with a strong cement

228

workers' union which is ever watchful of a bias that may occur in the distribution of value added in your firm between profit and wages, you probably will have to make some concessions to your employees before you increase your profit-taking. Incidentally, of course, economic theory has it that ideally only the first of the above three alternatives should take place, except that an innovator shall enjoy a temporary extra gain before the innovation becomes prevalent through competition. Thus, in pure theory, the benefit of innovation redounds to consumers in the form of reduced prices.

In fact, there was a time in United Kingdom, for example, when such expectation of pure theory was in a fair degree approximated. If you compare the nominal per capita income of U.K. between 1873 and 1893, it actually declined from £35.2 to £34.7. But if you adjust these figures for price changes and express them in real terms (in 1913–14 prices), it shows an increase of 35.4 percent from £28.8 to £39.0. As consumers, or as retired men living on fixed income, we would like to have this kind of situation prevail. Unfortunately, however, we no longer live in those golden days of *laissez faire* and have to put up with various institutional rigidities, so that nowadays technological innovations are seldom translated into the reduction of selling prices. In fact, it has become the generally accepted goal of monetary policy in all the western countries to aim at maintaining price stability, although a long-run price decline is what is consistent with continual technological progress.

Now, let us suppose that here is a manufacturing firm which has been able to raise its labour productivity by something like 12.2 percent per annum continually over the decade of the 1950's, while the market condition was such that the price of the product could be maintained at a stable level. You will say immediately that that firm must be in an enviable position of enjoying ample leeway in doing all kinds of things year after year, such as ploughing back, investing in research, giving bonuses to employees, etc. Especially is this the case if its competitors in the field succeeded in raising their labour pro- ductivities only at the annual rate of 2.3 percent to 5.8 percent at most. That firm in that enviable position was, in fact, the Japanese manufacturing industries taken as a whole; and the competitors referred to were those of U.K., the U.S.A., West Germany and France.

Price competition among countries, however, involves one important intermediate link, i.e. the exchange rate. If the exchange rate were adjusted continually, or even intermittently, according as differentials in cost reduction arise due to changing rates of productivity progress, international market equilibriun would not be disturbed. But, of course, no one proposes such a scheme; and in actual fact also the stable ratio has been the rule in the recent past. At least, Japan has not changed its exchange rate since April 1949 when the present ratio of 360 yen to a dollar, or 1,008 yen to a British pound was established.

Thus an important question arises here of how that ratio was determined. Though I refrain from going into technicalities on this occasion, two things are quite clear: (1) that an attempt was made to find a ratio equalizing the differing strengths, as it were, of yen and dollar at that time; and (2) that the Japanese economy in the spring of 1949 was still prostrate and functioning below its own potentialities. Three hundred and sixty yen to a dollar, in fact, seemed at the time a bit severe for Japan, but was certain to become within a year a lenient rate, since Japan was in the position of regaining its erstwhile strength while the U.S. and others had newly to improve upon their strength.

The situation was something like the case of a golf player who, let us say, used to have a handicap of 15 before a long illness, and upon recovery of health played a game with a colleague with the same handicap of 15, but showed unmistakably the effect of illness and was permitted to have his handicap raised to 24. This was to equalize the differing strengths at the time of the first game after his recovery. He, however, is now healthy; and since he once played as well as a man on a 15 handicap, he improves rapidly as he plays. Suppose he played another game with the same colleague with the handicap of 24 against 15; he would easily win. In the game of golf, I presume, the usual thing to do in such circumstances is to lower that gentleman's handicap as he demonstrates a definite sign of improvement. In the matter of exchange rates we do not do this necessarily. More important, not only do we not do it, but the economics of the case is such that what happens is as if the convalescent golfer could utilize somehow the winning margin of scores due to his bigger handicap in enabling himself to improve his game.

This golfer simile, of course, simplifies the problem too much. But Japanese manufacturing industries subsequent to the setting up of the single exchange rate in 1949 were, in a sense, in a situation similar to this convalescent golfer. The index of productivity in manufacturing rose by 24 percent in 1949 compared with the preceding year, by 31 percent in 1950 against 1949, and again by 37 percent in 1951 against 1950. Since the exchange rate was fixed all this while, Japanese industries found it easier and easier to expand their export markets even with a slightly rising domestic price level. And, of course, the rising domestic price level, coincidental with the rapidly rising productivity, was a boon for industrial profit. As we all know, wages always lag in such circumstances. Thus what I called the leeway that could be utilized for plough-back and so on became generally quite ample. Some of this leeway might have been dissipated; but a large part of it was either made use of by industries themselves for further improving their productive set-up, or syphoned off into the government coffer as corporate taxes to be spent on the construction of social overhead capital, which after all, creates external economies for private industries. The profit rate realized being high and thus the plough-back high also, the expectation for future profit possibilities became naturally sanguine. Optimistic expectation becomes justified in reality by the very act taken on the basis of that expectation.

In the back of all this was the accumulation of all kinds of technological innovations developed by advanced countries during the period Japan had been isolated from the world, such as electronics, automation devices, petrochemicals, new synthetic materials, etc. The general level of technique in Japan was already high enough for these innovations to be absorbed into Japanese industries without much delay.

It was in this way that the high level of investment was maintained during the past decade, supporting the high rate of growth of real GNP and at the same time yielding an average rate of productivity rise as high as 12.2 percent per annum. In a word, the explanation for the remarkable rate of growth, during the period after the rehabilitation was more or less over, lay, above all, in the favourable handicap of the exchange rate set up at the time of convalescence, matched by the catching-up process in technological progress under the condition of domestic price stability.

232

V

I am not saying that what I have just said is the only explanation of the recent growth experience of Japan. There were a number of other factors which should not escape our attention but which I am not going to dwell upon here. For example, the windfall of the Korean incident is one. On that occasion, the so-called United Nations Forces used Japan as their base of operation; and 'special procurements', paid in dollars, constituted more than a third of Japan's gross receipts from abroad on goods and services during 1951–53. In absolute figures, they declined only gradually and recorded the sum of $542 million even in 1960, still more than 10 percent of Japan's gross receipts from abroad.

Then, there was an element of flexibility in the supply of labour force. The forced repatriation after the war brought back to the Japanese soil nearly five million people most of whom were able-bodied men. The immediate lack of employment opportunities on that occasion was cushioned in a characteristic Japanese way through the expansion of disguised unemployment in agriculture and small-scale industries and commercial shops. Subsequently, as the need for labour force rose rapidly, this source could be tapped and more recently a fresh abundant supply became available from the unusual hump of births in the immediate postwar years.

Nor can we dismiss lightly the positive role played by the government in Japan's growth process in the 'fifties. Government embarked quite early on a gigantic industry-financing programme through a number of governmental development corporations, as well as introducing numerous tax-exemption

233

or tax-relief measures aimed at specific industries and investment programmes. The legacy of wartime high tax rates,
which take time for eventual relaxation, has helped the government to enjoy relatively ample financial resources; and the level
of treasury investments and loans has lately been of a magnitude
fully comparable to the total retained income of corporations.
The government has made use of such resources quite effectively
now for one industry and now for another, shifting the emphasis as the circumstances demanded. The extent of corporate
tax relief, on the other hand, is indicated by the rising ratio in
the early 'fifties of the tax-exempt portion of corporate gross
profit to the retained income of corporations. While the
denominator itself expanded, the ratio rose from 9 percent in
1951 to 113 percent in 1952, 152 in 1953, and 213 in 1954.[5]
It appears to be certain that, were it not for such a sharing of
risk by the government, several of the essential industries would
not have achieved the level of investment that was recorded in
the 'fifties.

Profit rate was high, and governmental financial assistance
too was available. Nevertheless, the major portion of financial
resources for industrial firms came in the first instance from
commercial banks. Japanese industries traditionally depended
for their funds—not only for operating capital but also for fixed
capital—upon loans from commercial banks. This used to be
explained partly in terms of a high rate of saving by the public,
who would deposit their money in saving-type accounts of
banks, and partly also in terms of the peculiarly Japanese
monopoly structure called 'Zaibatsu', each one of which
encompassed banking as well as manufacturing and trade, and

[5] See Economic Planning Agency, *Sengo Nihon no Shihon Chikuseki to Kigyo Keiei*,
1957, p. 156.

had good reason to feel that even a long-term lending for a risky venture was a matter within one's own family, so to speak.

This peculiarity of industrial firms depending on banks even for their long-term investment funds is, if at all, more marked in the postwar Japan than in the pre-war. A recent comparative study[6] shows that, whereas in the United States of all the sources of financial funds for corporations including retained income only 5.8 percent was accounted for by loans from banks, such a ratio was as high as 31.6 percent in Japan. Even in West Germany, which like Japan has the tradition of high dependence on banks, the ratio was 18.8 percent. It is still true that the personal rate of saving is high in Japan and people make use of banks as depository of their savings. The practice of biased financing to firms related by 'Zaibatsu' ties has also been revived. But the scale of credit expansion which we have witnessed in recent years calls for an additional explanation. The ultimate provider of credit to commercial banks is the central bank; and the volume of central bank credit outstanding relative to the scale of economic activities gives us an indication of the degree of credit inflation. Since the total volume of bank notes in circulation has kept roughly a constant proportion with national income, we might compare the volume of central bank credit outstanding with the total volume of currency at the same point of time for different years. In the typical pre-war years, in the late 'thirties for example, the former stood at the level of about one-third to one-fourth compared with the latter. (You must remember, of course, that the late 'thirties was already a semi-war period for Japan.) After 1950, however, such a ratio started to rise, at first to the

---

[6] Sogo Seisaku Kenkyukai, *Nihon no Setsubi Toshi*, 1963, pp. 46–9. The period covered is the latter half of 1950's.

40 percent level in 1951–54 and then to more than 50 percent after 1957; and for the first time in the history of Japan it crossed over the 100 level in 1961.

How did it come about? The level of central bank credit, of course, is the net result of all kinds of factors, some of which are policy-oriented. But in a large measure it reflects the volume of commercial bank credit in general; and the latter could not be too far out of line with the scale of economic activities as a whole. In other words, if stated in the simplest manner, there should be here a chain of proportional relations: the central bank credit outstanding is proportional to the volume of commercial bank credit which in turn is proportional to the scale of economic activities which again in turn is proportional to the currency in circulation. But we have seen that the proportion between the first and the last items in this chain has not been maintained—in fact, it shifted sharply upwards. There must be, therefore, a break in the chain somewhere. Where could it be?

One plausible hypothesis is that the credit structure has been over-expanded relative to the scale of recorded economic activities in recent years and has played the role of a powerful bellows in expanding investment and other activities. But, after all, an over-expansion of credit would be short-lived unless it obtained substantive support from the realm of credit-worthy factors of some kind.

It is my opinion that there has recently been available such a credit-worthy factor in Japan; and that is the steadily and sharply rising price of land, a phenomenon which is most characteristic of a country like Japan. New, let me give you an example. I bought a piece of residential land in Tokyo in 1951, paying the price of ¥2500 per *tsubo*, or a unit of land measure in

Japan which is 6 feet by 6. Since 1951, the wholesale price level in Japan has been more or less stable up to now. If I sell this piece of land today, I can fetch a price of ¥250,000 per *tsubo*, i.e. exactly one hundred times! The rise of 100 times over the last 13 years is not an exception. Many of the factory sites now available, even outside city limits, cost ¥10,000 per *tsubo* or more, so that one hectare (2.47 acres) of land would cost 30 million yen (30 thousand British pounds) or more. More paradoxical is the situation which a rice cultivating farmer faces today. On one hectare of land, the average crop he can expect would be 30 *koku* (10,000 pounds) of husked rice which can be sold to the government at the total value of 450,000 yen. If we subtract from this the cost of fertilizers, etc. amounting to, let us say, 15 percent, the farmer's net revenue (including, of course, the equivalent of his labour income) would be a little less than 400,000 yen. Apply the conversion interest rate of 6 percent, and you obtain the capitalized value of the land (plus toil) of about 6.5 million yen. Compare this with the price which he could fetch if he were to sell the land to one of these factories, i.e. 30 million yen. You can easily sympathize with a farmer who gives up farming and decides to live on the interest income.

In fact, many pieces of land changed ownership in the past ten years, and tremendous capital gains were realized. Capital gains, however, are essentially transfer income. They go into some one's pocket and of course can be used for any purpose one likes, but they have to come out of some one else's pocket, paid not in return for an addition to current production, but in return for a change in the title to what existed before. Gross national product is not affected in any way by a mere change in the title of ownership. Yes, theoretically, that is the case. But in actual fact, something does happen. First of all, the real

237

estate business has become a tremendously thriving one supporting a large number of persons out of the funds which are
nothing but a transfer. Their incomes, of course, do constitute
a part of gross national product. Then, characteristically
enough, sellers of land nowadays are, more often than not,
private persons including farmers who will consider their
proceeds as funds for present and future consumption, whereas
buyers of land are, more often than not, corporations and other
business concerns which borrow money in order to buy land
and after gaining the title of ownership are in the position to
borrow money again on the strength of their ownership of the
land. Land is a credit-worthy object, and the higher the price
is, the more credit is forthcoming. In other words, the money
to buy land comes from bank credit and the money received is
destined to consumption; or one may say, at the risk of oversimplification, bank credit is created to support additional
consumption. At the same time, the ownership of land as the
basis of obtaining credit (this is relevant usually only to business
concerns) has multiplied its impact almost 100 times within 13
years or so while the wholesale price level has remained stable.

I believe that this boom in land prices, which is less due to
speculation than to stress in the supply-and-demand situation,
has been an important factor in the credit expansion of the past
decade. It was at once a product of rapid economic growth
and a supporting pillar for the needed credit expansion for that
rapid economic growth.

VI

However we may explain it, the fact of Japan's rapid economic
growth cannot be denied; and many of my countrymen take

satisfaction in this fact. But I am inclined to view this whole question a bit more philosophically.

First of all, whenever I think of this problem of price boom in land, I am reminded of a story which the older generation of Japanese often like to tell. It is a story of two happy-go-lucky fellows, you might say. Let us call them John and Peter. It was a season of flower-viewing in Japan when common people go out on a picnic to parks where cherry-blossoms are in full bloom and have a good time, singing, drinking and shouting at each other hilariously. Both John and Peter wanted to join such festivity; but unfortunately, they were practically penniless. All they had between them was a fifty-yen coin which was barely sufficient to buy just one glass of *sake*, Japanese rice wine. But they thought of a grand idea of buying on credit from a *sake*-dealer a cask of *sake*, to be paid at the end of the day. Their idea was to transport the cask to a park and sell *sake* to the flower-viewing crowd while they too enjoyed the occasion in the crowd. The cost of *sake* per glass was for them 40 yen, but they thought of selling it at 50 yen which would be reasonable enough. Thus they started out, carrying the cask on a pole, John holding the front end and Peter the rear. Peter, who kept in his pocket their common asset of 50 yen, could not resist, as they walked, the aroma of *sake* floating towards him on the breeze, so he spoke to John who was in the front:

'Hey, John! This *sake* is for business, I know. So I am not going to ask for a free drink. But if I pay for it, it's all right, isn't it?'

'Of course, Peter. So long as it's paid for, it makes no difference who drinks it.' Thus Peter had a glass of *sake* and paid for it with the 50–yen coin he had in his pocket. Now

John had the 50–yen coin; and as they were about to start trekking again, John too felt an urge:

'Hey, Peter!' he said, 'How about selling me a glass, too?'

'It's all right, so long as you pay for it.'

'Here is your 50 yen, then.'

Now the coin was transferred to Peter. Another 100 yards they went, and Peter smelled the aromatic breeze again and asked to 'buy' a glass, reciprocated subsequently by John. And this was repeated time and again. By the time they reached the destination, the cask was empty and all the money they had was the same 50–yen coin and not a penny more.

The lesson of this story is clear. While the transfer of money was taking place between them ostentatiously as purchase and sale, a cask of *sake* was gone and the debt to the *sake* dealer remained unpaid. Transfer of land from one hand to another at ever higher prices in Japan has cost something to the Japanese economy without creating any new product. The net cost involved for the economy as a whole may be small. But what is an apparent cost for the economy is a real cost for industrial firms, expressing itself as the cost of acquiring factory sites, which constitute an item of comparative disadvantage for Japanese industries in international competition. There is also another aspect to the high cost of land which we cannot ignore. That is, the inordinate disproportion which has arisen between the price of land and the prices of ordinary goods produced has made it difficult to execute a rational plan of urban redevelopment and highway construction. Even when the benefit estimated from a certain plan of urban redevelopment is fairly high, it is often the case that the high cost of land purchase cannot be compensated for by the benefit expressed in value terms.

Many firms could afford the high price of factory sites because of the ample leeway in their earnings, which I discussed before; and in consequence, they kept on bidding up the price. And now we are confronted with a peculiarly iniquitous situation involving all kinds of real, apparent, and opportunity costs. The important thing here is that all this is not an unavoidable cost. Land is valuable in Japan. There is no question about it. But it could be easily foreseen that with the progress of urbanization and mushrooming of many new factories the serious strain would converge upon this one resource which cannot be expanded in supply except in a most negligible measure. Foresight in this regard would have made it possible to work out a plan of rational allocation combined with equitable control over the price of transfer. I would say, it is not yet too late to embark upon such a programme.

VII

The problem of land boom illustrates another important aspect of the so-called rapid economic growth; that is the sobering aspect of the use of such a measure as national income or GNP as the index of economic welfare. The land boom did have the effect of raising Japan's national income; but did it increase the economic welfare of the Japanese people? That is the question.

It is very often taken for granted that the bigger the national income, the bigger the economic welfare; and that the bigger the economic welfare, the bigger the general wellbeing of the nation as a whole. I have always doubted simple proportionality of this kind; but, having observed at first hand the process of raipd economic growth in Japan during the past decade, I have become convinced that a definite warning is now in order.

241

Let me give you what may appear to be a rather extreme example. Let us suppose, quite hypothetically of course, that here are two communities, A and B. We shall assume that they are exactly alike, in the industries they have, the distribution of of income, the number of unemployed, and even as regards such matters as that mosquitoes are unknown to both communities. The community income would be the same in such circumstances. Let us say, each has one hundred people unemployed. And here we introduce an assumption with respect to which A differs from B. In the community A, those 100 unemployed keep on trying their best to find a job in a legitimate fashion, so to speak, by frequenting employment exchanges or retraining themselves as best as they can. In the community B, however, those 100 unemployed, we assume, get together one day and discuss what they as a group might be able to do by themselves. There is a shrewd fellow among them who proposes an idea. He says something like this to the group: 'Fellows! You may not know, but I hear that there is what is known as "mosquitoes" in this world. They multiply in the summer time and, as I understand it, they are extremely annoying. In those places where they still have mosquitoes, people consider mosquito-nets and mosquito-incensecoils as daily necessities. Now, fellows, my idea is: we borrow money from a bank; and several of us will travel to the country where they still have mosquitoes and bring them back, while the rest of us will set up a factory manufacturing mosquito-nets and coils. I am certain that we will succeed. How about it?' They all vote affirmatively and immediately proceed with the plan. Mosquitoes are duly brought back and spread all over the community. Citizens start to complain, but, fortunately, mosquito-nets and coils are at hand on the market; and the

242

annoyance can be alleviated. And, of course, the unemployment disappears in the community B. When economists
calculate community income of A and B at the end of the
year, the community B is found to have a higher income
than the community A.

Can we say in this case, that economic welfare of B is higher
than that of A? I doubt it very much. But some of you may
say that that was an extremely unrealistic example.

The fact of the matter is that an occurrence of this nature is
not so uncommon in some of the societies we know. There is a
famous story of the sale of potato peelers in the United States.
Makers of potato peelers noticed a puzzling fact at one time that
although potato peelers never wear out, enough are sold in two
years in the United States to put one in every home. So there
was an investigation which revealed that they got thrown away
with potato peelings. Having found this out, one of the makers
came up with a dazzling plan for helping along this throwaway
process. The proposal was that the company paint its peelers
with a colour 'as much like a potato peeling as possible.' This
was done. But since a potato-coloured peeler would not have
much eye appeal on the sales counter, they solved this problem
by displaying the peeler on a colourful card. Once the house-
wife got the peeler home and removed the bright card, the
chances that she would lose the peeler were excellent. The
man who thought of this dazzling plan proudly said: 'Next
year we expect to double our sales.'[7]

Probably, they did succeed in doubling their sales and
thereby contributed to the growth of U.S. national income.
But we can hardly call this addition to national income an
addition to economic welfare. Examples of this kind can be

[7] The story is related in V. Packard, *The Waste Makers*, 1960, pp. 47–8.

multiplied; but more relevant to the case of recent Japan would be an example like the doubling of traffic policemen in Tokyo, which, though it undoubtedly had the effect of increasing Japan's national income, is nothing but a reflection of the lack of foresight in city planning and of the recklessness or immaturity of drivers in Tokyo. It is a paradox that avoidable cost to the community of this kind is a cause for the expansion of community income.

The single-tracked emphasis on 'income doubling' which has characterized the recent Japan is somewhat similar to emphasizing the speed of a car as it drives through a narrow, muddy road. The faster it runs, the more satisfied may be the driver and actually the more applause he receives from certain quarters. But there are pedestrians who have to lean flat on the house-wall on the road-side and yet cannot escape from the mud splashed by the fast driving car. The damage on the clothes is not counted as a negative item in the national economic accounts; in fact, it may well be registered on the positive side if the victim sends his dirtied clothes to the laundry, thus 'creating income'. The simile is especially appropriate to Japan where the land space is narrow relative to the number of population, and any expansion of industrial activities gets into conflict with those citizen interests which are usually treated as outside the economic calculation. The best example in this regard is provided by the mounting instances of public nuisance.

Take, for example, the case of the city of Yokkaichi facing the bay of Ise not far from the city of Nagoya in the central part of Japan. Yokkaichi started out as a port city in the modern Japan, combined with a scenic bathing beach. It is now one of the biggest centres of Japan's petro-chemical industry.

244

When the city was chosen as the factory site for the petro-chemical industry about a decade ago, it was evident then that there was not enough space for all the allied and associated plants to be built at a convenient location. Thus a gigantic piece of reclamation work was done along the scenic sea shore. But neither the residential section along the sea shore nor the congested urban centre near the port facilities was moved. The result is that one of the best residential sections, in fact the one constructed by Yokkaichi municipality, has now lost the scenic view of the bay and is separated from a huge thermal electric plant only by a narrow strip of road.   Residents of that section suffer, day and night, from what they call 'vibratory noise.'   Again, almost all residents of the older part of the city suffer from air pollution; and many have succumbed to respira-tory diseases.   Then, there is a fishing village nearby where the oil-soaked dirty water is drained and the stench damage on fish caught has now become so serious that the fishing industry there is on the way out.   Yokkaichi now is a city which pays the highest per capita tax to the central government among all the cities in Japan (about 200,000 yen per annum) and the mammoth petro-chemical industry plants are buzzing 24 hours a day.   And as might be expected, these big newcomers built company residences for their employees far out on the hillside, whence company buses carry them back and forth.   But the old citizens of Yokkaichi are like pedestrians on a narrow, muddy road.   Their welfare had decidedly suffered, but economic statisticians tell them that their average per capita income has risen.   Probably more than any other country, Japan will have to face up with the problem of public nuisance in the modern age.

In a small country with a large population with a long

245

cultural history, any act of large scale reorganisation in land use is likely to be confronted with a dilemma of construction of the new and destruction of the old.   For almost any site you choose for the construction of highways, of factories, or of new residential agglomeration, you are likely to find historic remains, beautiful old trees four hundred years old, etc.   These are *priceless* things—priceless in the double sense of the term, i.e. firstly, they are so valuable that no price can be attached and secondly they are not priced in any way when they are lost. Because they are not priced when they are lost, the 'income-doubling'-minded people apparently think nothing of them. Thus occurs that paradoxical phenomenon: 'construction destroys'.   Those of you who have been in Japan may have visited in Tokyo a park known as the 'Educational Park of Nature'.   It occupies an area within the so-called 'ring' as big as 20 hectares (or about 50 acres) and is the only natural forest area—other than the Imperial Palace grounds—preserving the rustic beauty of the old Tokyo plain.   Enter there, and you will see a row of a hundred pasania trees 400 years old among others, and enjoy the restful atmosphere with the chirping of many a bird usually not heard in a city like Tokyo. The value of this park for the citizens of Tokyo, I would say, is incalculable.   And yet, the imperative of 'construction' has dictated the splitting of this park into halves by letting a speed highway run through the middle.   When such a plan was announced by the government, a protest from citizens immediately arose; and finally, a compromise was reached to make the highway skirt on the edge but inside the park instead of splitting it.   Even this compromise cannot but cause some damage to the park, what with the exhaust fumes from cars, what with the noises, not to speak of some of the trees that are being sacrificed. The construction *cum* destruction is going on just now; and many of us Tokyo citizens pass by the place with a dreary awareness of irreparable loss. Such is the price we pay for the miracle of 'income-doubling in a decade.'

Surely, you will agree with me that the growth of national income is not necessarily proportional to the growth of economic welfare, and further that the growth of economic welfare is not necessarily proportional to the increase of welfare in general.

VIII

It may be said that I have overstepped my bounds as an economist in laying so much stress on what are usually considered to be noneconomic factors. But after all, economics, which is presumably a science concerned with the instruments with which we enhance our human welfare, is still a very imperfect science. The frontiers of the science are never closed; and I should like to feel that in time we shall be able to deal, within a systematic framework of our discipline, with such problems as public nuisance, so that the balance sheet which economic statisticians will present will not be confined to the market valuation of goods sold and bought. The experience of the unusually rapid economic growth of Japan, to me, is a reminder that our science is still not remotely equal to the task of giving answers to the questions which welfare-minded laymen might ask.

But let me conclude by coming back to the narrower, more immediate problem of prognosis on the prospect of economic growth in Japan. If my earlier analysis is correct, that is, the explanation in terms of the catching-up process under the given exchange rate set up when Japan was still a convalescent, it follows that there will inevitably come a time when the impetus thus created will be consumed. The catching-up process, after all, is something which happens only once. Now, however, I have to be more specific about the meaning of this term. It is clear that the catching-up process of Japan consisted of two parts: one is the catching-up with Japan's *own* potentialities— this aspect was quite significant because the long drawn-out war and the prostration subsequent to her defeat kept Japan's industrial performance below her own par for some time; the other is the catching-up with the advanced level of western countries. Of these two aspects, there seems to be little doubt that the former ended several years back—most probably around the middle of the 'fifties or a little later. The latter, on the other hand, is, in a sense, a perpetual process. That is to say, Japan may never catch up with the United States in a foreseeable future. Suppose this were the case, i.e. against the U.S. performance of 100 at any time, Japan's performance remained at 90, although both countries are assumed to be making progress continually. The question is: has Japan attained that relative performance level of 90 already, or is she still around, say, 70 or 80? It is not possible, of course, to give an unequivocal answer to this kind of question; but again I venture to guess that we have not yet come to that impenetrable wall of 90 but are possibly nearer to 70 than to 80. In other words, the annual rate of productivity rise of Japan is likely to be higher than that of the United States still for a number of years to come. But, by the nature of the case, the gap in the rate of growth between these two countries will become smaller and smaller as Japan approaches that hypothetical wall of 90. That is to say, if the U.S. productivity is going to rise at the annual rate of 2 per cent, Japan may yet be able to raise her

248

productivity annually by 3 or 4 percent, but certainly not by 7 or 8 percent as she has been doing in the recent past.

The Japanese government has just worked out a so-called 'middle-range' plan, extending over the next five years, envisaging an average annual growth rate of GNP of 9 percent. This, as you remember, is approximately the rate at which Japan has been growing during the past 15 years or so. It is my considered judgement that this is over-ambitious, even aside from the question which I admubrated earlier with a simile of a fast-driving car on a narrow, muddy road.

In particular, there are four problems which will become increasingly important from now on as Japan tries to maintain a high rate of growth. (1) Since Japan is a peculiarly foreign-trade oriented country, unable to avoid dependence on foreign supplies for essential raw materials for her industries, her exports will have to expand at least at the same rate as the growth rate of the economy as a whole. Here is *the balance of payments problem*. (2) Fresh supply of labour force will still be numerically ample until 1966 or '67; but the bottlenecks have begun to appear here and there, causing a shift upwards of the wage scale in general. Thus from now on, it will become increasingly important to break the peculiarly Japanese institutional barriers against labour mobility. Here is the problem of *labour force supply and labour mobility*. (3) The rapid rise of productivity in a specific industry tends to bring about a proportional rise in money wage rate in that industry. Such wage rise tends to spread to those industries where productivity does not rise as much, thus causing a price rise. This is especially true in service industries, including government service. Since there is a tendency for the productivity-rising industries to be characterized by administered prices, the net

249

result is a constantly rising trend of consumer prices. A similar tendency is shared more or less by other western countries and thus far the relative position of Japan has not been especially impaired. But can we hope for the same in the future? I am not quite sure. In other words, here is a problem of *rising prices*. (4) It cannot be doubted that the social overhead structures, providing external economies for the private sector, will demand a greater share of the total capital needs in the future. This is a cost for the society, making demands on public funds either to be provided for by tax revenues or by government borrowing. In other words, using the same old simile again, the task ahead for Japan is less that of increasing the speed of the car than that of widening and paving the road. Here, then, is the problem of providing the so-called *infrastructure*.

When we consider these problems I have just mentioned, it appears to me to be clear that what Japan needs today is what we might call 'a balanced growth'. In this sense, although our government is rather reluctant to admit it, we are now at a turning point.

INDEX OF NAMES

INDEX OF NAMES

INDEX OF SUBJECTS

INDEX OF SUBJECTS

INDEX OF SUBJECTS